W9-BSF-454

The Christian's Secret of a Happy Life for Today

A PARAPHRASE OF HANNAH WHITALL SMITH'S CLASSIC

CATHERINE JACKSON

Published for the
Billy Graham Evangelistic Association

by

world wide
publications

1303 Hennepin Avenue,
Minneapolis, Minnesota 55403

Unless otherwise identified Scripture quotations are based on the King James Version of the Bible.

Scripture quotations identified RSV are from the Revised Standard Version of the Bible, copyrighted 1946, 1952, © 1971 and 1973.

Scripture quotations identified NEB are from The New English Bible. © The Delegates of the Oxford University Press and the Syndics of the Cambridge University Press 1961 and 1970. Reprinted by permission.

Scripture quotations identified LB are from The Living Bible, Copyright © 1971 by Tyndale House Publishers, Wheaton, Illinois 60187. All rights reserved.

Scripture quotations identified PHILLIPS are from THE NEW TESTAMENT IN MODERN ENGLISH (Revised Edition), translated by J. B. Phillips. © J. B. Phillips 1958, 1960, 1972. Used by permission of Macmillan Publishing Co., Inc.

Scripture quotations identified TEV are from the *Good News Bible*—Old Testament: Copyright © American Bible Society 1976. New Testament: Copyright © American Bible Society 1966, 1971, 1976.

Ornaments indicate omissions of a paragraph or more from the original.

Library of Congress Cataloging in Publication Data

Jackson, Catherine.
    The Christian's secret of a happy life for today.

    1. Christian life—1960—   2. Faith. I. Smith
Hannah Whitall, 1832-1911.   The Christian's secret of a
happy life. II. Title.
BV4501.2.J3125   248'.4   78-9896
ISBN-0-8007-0976-4

Copyright © 1979 by Catherine Jackson
Published by Fleming H. Revell Company
All rights reserved
Printed in the United States of America

TO Mary Lynch, who has always known the secret,
and to Ed, who helped me to learn it

Contents

Preface

This is not a theological book. I admit at the beginning that I have never studied theology and don't even understand its terms. But the Lord has taught me through experience some truths about Himself and His relations to us that have helped me a great deal. I believe these truths could help others, and I feel it would be wrong to keep them a personal secret.

I don't want to change any Christian's theological views. The truths I have to share aren't theological in any sense; they are simply practical. I believe they are the basic truths of life and experience which underlie all theology. They will make it possible for those who have accepted Christ as their Savior to experience the reality of His presence in their own lives.

Obedience is the key to the mastery of any subject—whether art, science, or religion. If any person learns from this book how to obey Jesus better, that person will discover something of the secret I am trying to share.

I have committed this book to the Lord and have asked Him to erase from the reader's memory anything in it that is wrong, and to let only the truths it contains speak to anyone. It is sent out in sympathy and love for all Christians who are struggling and weary of the struggle, and its message goes straight from my heart to theirs.

I pray that Jesus Himself may use it as a means of teaching some of His followers the true secret of a happy life.

H.W.S.

1
Is It Scriptural?

An agnostic once said to me, "You Christians seem to have a religion that makes you miserable. You are like a man with a headache. He doesn't want to get rid of his head, but it hurts him to keep it. Surely you don't expect me to give up my way of living for such an uncomfortable faith."

That remark stung me and made me realize, for the first time, that the Christian faith ought to be, and was *meant* to be, something to make its followers happy, not miserable. Then and there I began to ask the Lord to show me the secret of a happy Christian life. This is the secret that I shall try to tell in the following pages.

Maybe you are one of the large number of believers whose experience of the Christian life has been disappointing. You have accepted Jesus as your Savior, but you don't know Him as the source of your very life. You have tried to serve God and advance His Kingdom; you have carefully studied the Bible and have learned many precious truths from it—truths which you have tried to put into practice. But all this knowledge and all your church activities aren't satisfying you. You are still hungry and thirsty. In fact, you are starving for that bread, that water of life, which the Scriptures promise to all believers. In the very depths of your heart, you know that your religion is only empty words compared to what the early Christians enjoyed, possessed, and lived in. You have finally decided that the best you can expect from your faith is an endless cycle of alternate failures and victories: sinning, repenting, and beginning again—only to sin again, repent again, and begin again once more.

11

But *is* this all? When Jesus laid down His life to deliver you from your bondage to Satan, did He intend to give you only *partial* deliverance—to leave you struggling with defeat and discouragement? Did He fear that continuous victory would somehow dishonor Him?

And all those prophecies and confident statements concerning the coming of the Messiah and the work He was to accomplish—did they mean no more than this partial victory? Did each promise have a catch to it that was meant to prevent its complete fulfillment?

"Being delivered out of the hand of our enemies" (Luke 1:74). Does that mean only a few of them?

Causing us "always . . . to triumph in Christ" (2 Corinthians 2:14). Does "always" mean *some*times?

"More than conquerors through him that loved us" (Romans 8:37). Do conquerors experience constant defeat and failure?

The answer to all these questions is a resounding *no!* Jesus is able to save us *fully* and *completely* (Hebrews 7:25 PHILLIPS), and He means to do so. God's promise, confirmed by His oath, was that he would ". . . rescue us from our enemies and allow us to serve him without fear, so that we might be holy and righteous before him all the days of our life" (Luke 1:74, 75 TEV). It is an awesome task but our Deliverer is able to do it. He came to "destroy the works of the devil" (1 John 3:8). Do we dare believe that He is either unable or unwilling to accomplish what He set out to do?

At the very beginning, then, you can be sure of this: that Jesus came to save you fully—now, in this life—from the power of sin, and to rescue you altogether from your spiritual enemies. Every scriptural declaration concerning the purpose of His death on the cross states that His work is to deliver us from our sins and from the *power* of sin. Not a hint is given anywhere that this deliverance is to be only the partial one experienced by most Christians.

When the angel of the Lord appeared to Joseph in a dream and announced the coming birth of the Savior, he said, ". . . and you shall call his name Jesus, for he will save his people from their sins" (Matthew 1:21 RSV).

After Peter had healed the lame beggar in the porch of the temple, he preached to the Jews who had witnessed the miraculous healing. He concluded his sermon by saying, "God, having raised up his Son Jesus, sent him to bless you, in turning away every one of you from his iniquities" (Acts 3:26).

Paul told the Christians at Ephesus that Jesus' purpose in laying down His life for the church was "to make her holy, having cleansed her through the baptism of his Word—to make her an altogether glorious Church in his eyes. She is to be free from spots, wrinkles or any other disfigurement—a Church holy and perfect" (Ephesians 5:26, 27 PHILLIPS). Those who criticize Christianity as a religion that promises "pie in the sky by and by" don't realize that the Scriptures have far more to say about *present* salvation from sin than about a *future* salvation in heaven. In writing Titus about the grace of God, Paul explained what that grace does for us: ". . . by it we are disciplined to renounce godless ways and worldly desires, and to live a life of temperance, honesty, and godliness *in the present age*" (Titus 2:12 NEB, italics added). Then he added that the reason Jesus sacrificed Himself for us was ". . . to set us free from all wickedness and to make us a

pure people marked out for his own, eager to do good"
(Titus 2:14 NEB).

Peter told the Christians to whom he was writing that
Christ suffered for them, leaving them an example,
". . . that you should follow in his steps. He committed
no sin; no guile was found on his lips . . . . He himself
bore our sins in his body on the tree, that we might die to
sin and live to righteousness. By his wounds you have been
healed" (1 Peter 2:21, 22, 24 RSV).

In the sixth chapter of Romans, Paul answered forever
the question of a Christian's continuing in sin: "God forbid." (v. 2). "We know that the man we once were has been
crucified with Christ, for the destruction of the sinful self,
so that we may no longer be the slaves of sin" (v. 6 NEB).

Can we honestly think for one moment that our holy
God, who hates sin in the sinner, is willing to put up with it
in the Christian? Would He have arranged a plan of salvation which saved us only from the *guilt* of sin and not from
its *power*? With Paul I say, "God forbid!" The redemption
accomplished for us at Calvary is a redemption from the
power of sin as well as from its guilt. Jesus *is* able to
". . . save fully and completely those who approach God
through him . . ." (Hebrews 7:25 PHILLIPS).

The following thoughts are adapted from those of a
Quaker writer.

There is nothing so contrary to God as sin, and
God will not allow sin always to rule His master-
piece, man. When we consider God's infinite

power for destroying that which is contrary to Him, who can believe that the devil must always stand and prevail? Such a belief is inconsistent with true faith.

No man can redeem himself, and no man can live without sin. That is true. But I cannot accept the doctrine that God's power is unable to redeem us out of sin, that it is impossible for God to do it because the devil doesn't like it. I cannot accept that anyone has to remain in bondage to sin because the devil has such a power over him that God cannot set him free! This is deplorable doctrine; yet is *has* been preached.

Isn't man God's creature? Can't He make him new and cast sin out of him? Sin is deeply rooted in man, to be sure—yet not so deeply rooted that Jesus is unable to destroy it and to make man righteous and holy. We must throw away the Bible if we say that God cannot deliver man out of sin.

If a child of yours was kidnapped, you would gladly pay the ransom required for his release. But you would feel terribly cheated if you paid the ransom and he remained a captive—even though he might be *called* a "redeemed captive."

It is bad enough for one's body to be in captivity—but much worse to have one's soul held prisoner by Satan. Jesus said, ". . . every one who commits sin is a slave to sin" (John 8:34 RSV). If I have sinned, I am a slave, a captive who must be redeemed out of captivity. I cannot pay the price for myself, but Jesus has paid the price for

me. He is my Redeemer, and I shall expect to
come out of my captivity. If you tell me that I
must abide in sin as long as I live—that there is no
getting free from sin—I will ask, "What sort of
redemption is this? How does it help me in this
life?"

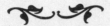

Please don't reject the idea of total victory over sin until
you have prayerfully searched the Scriptures to see
whether they support this doctrine. As you search, ask
God to enlighten you by His Spirit,

> . . . so that you may know what is the hope to
> which he calls you, what the wealth and glory of
> the share he offers you among his people in their
> heritage, and how vast the resources of his power
> open to us who trust in him. They are measured
> by his strength and the might which he exerted in
> Christ when he raised him from the dead, when
> he enthroned him at his right hand in the
> heavenly realms.
>
> Ephesians 1:18–20 NEB

When you begin to have some faint glimpses of the vast
resources of God's power, look away from your own weakness and put yourself and your problems entirely into His
hands, trusting Him to deliver you.

> When you take the field against an enemy and
> are faced by horses and chariots and an army
> greater than yours, do not be afraid of them; for

the Lord your God, who brought you out of Egypt, will be with you. When you are about to join battle, the priest shall come forward and address the army in these words: "Hear, O Israel, this day you are joining battle with the enemy; do not lose heart, or be afraid, or give way to panic in face of them; for the Lord your God will go with you to fight your enemy for you and give you the victory."

Deuteronomy 20:1–4 NEB

2

God's Side and Man's Side

The higher Christian life—which I also call the life of faith, the life of trust, the walk of faith, the life that is "hid with Christ in God" (Colossians 3:3), or just plain "sanctification"—has two sides: God's side and man's side. Because many people think it has only one side to it, there is a great deal of misunderstanding about it.

Put simply, God's part is to *work;* man's part is to *trust.* Although these two parts are quite distinct from each other, they are not really contradictory.

What is the work to be accomplished by God? It is to deliver us from the power of sin and to make us "perfect in every good work to do his will" (Hebrews 13:21). We are to be changed by the Holy Spirit into the very image of Christ (2 Corinthians 3:18; Romans 8:29).

This is real work! Bad habits have to be overcome. Negative emotions have to be rooted out and replaced with positive ones. In other words, a complete transformation has to take place.

Now *somebody* must do this work. Either we must do it for ourselves, or Someone else must do it for us. Most of us try to do it for ourselves at first and fail completely. If we turn to the Bible, we find the reason for our failure. We discover that we aren't even *supposed* to be able to do this work for ourselves. This is the work that Jesus has come to do for us, and He *will* do it for all who put themselves entirely in His hands and *trust* Him to do it.

The part of the believer, then, is to trust; it is the Lord, in whom he trusts, who actually does the work.

Trusting and *doing* are certainly contrasting and often contradictory ideas. If I said of one party in a transaction that he trusted a business matter to another and yet attended to it himself, I would be making a contradictory statement. But when I say of *two* parties in a transaction that one trusts the other to do something and that the second party then goes to work and does it, the two statements are perfectly harmonious. To say that man's part in the higher Christian life is to trust and God's part is to do the thing entrusted to Him is surely not contradictory and should not be puzzling.

The statement that man's part in the life of faith consists only of surrender and trust is often criticized, because it seems to say that believers should sit down in a sort of religious easy chair and make no effort to accomplish anything. Such a criticism may be justified if the other side of the matter isn't made clear: that when *we* trust, the *Lord* works. God always responds to our faith by accomplishing that which we entrust to Him.

Statements emphasizing God's part in the higher Christian life are also subject to criticism, on the ground that they say nothing about trust. The Lord's part is not to trust but to work—to do the thing entrusted to Him. He disciplines and trains us by inward impressions and outward circumstances. With all wisdom and all love, He refines and purifies us. Everything in the life and circumstances of the trusting believer is made to serve the one great purpose of making him, day by day and hour by hour, more like Jesus. This process of transformation may be long or short, depending upon the individual involved; but eventually it brings about the results for which the believer has trusted God.

Suppose, for instance, that a Christian dares by faith to "reckon," or regard himself as dead to sin, according to the command in Romans 6:11. The Lord makes this reckoning a reality, putting the natural man to death by a thousand little chastenings. What the Christian believes becomes his actual experience because God makes it so. Yet if we dwell *only* upon God's processes for turning faith's reckoning into reality, we may seem to set before the believer an impossible and hopeless task—that of sanctifying himself by works.

Sanctification—a theological term for the development of Christlikeness, or Christ's likeness, in the believer's life and character—*is both an instant step of faith and a gradual process of works.* Our part is the step; God's part is the process. By a *step* of faith we enter into the life of Jesus; by a *process* we are made to "grow up into him in all things" (Ephesians 4:15). By a step of faith we put ourselves into the hands of the divine Potter; by a gradual process He makes us into vessels that are suitable for His use.

Suppose I was describing to you the way in which a lump of clay is made into a vase. I would tell you first that the only thing the clay has to do is just lie passive in the potter's hands, submitting itself to all he does to it. There is really nothing else to be said about the clay's part. But if you have an inquiring mind, you would then say to me, "Yes, I see what the clay must do. But what about the potter?"

My reply would be, "That's the important part. The potter takes the clay and begins to knead and work it, tearing it apart and pressing it together again, wetting it and then letting it dry. Sometimes he works at it for hours; then he may lay it aside for days. When all this work has made it perfectly pliable in his hands, he proceeds to shape it into the vase he has in mind. He turns it on the wheel, planes it and smoothes it, dries it in the sun, and bakes it in the oven. When he finally turns it out of his workshop, it is a beautiful vase, perfectly suited to the purpose he had in mind."

The clay has nothing to do but lie passive in the potter's hands; it did not have to make itself into a vase. The clay's part and the potter's part are necessarily *contrasting* but not in the least *contradictory*. The clay is not expected to do the potter's work, but only to submit to his working.

Equally clear, it seems to me, is the perfect harmony between the two contrasting aspects of sanctification. The only thing to be said about man's part in this great work is that he must continually surrender himself and continually trust. But when we come to God's part, it is impossible to describe the many and varied ways in which He accomplishes the work entrusted to Him.

This is where the growing comes in. The lump of clay would never grow into a vase if it stayed in the clay pit for thousands of years. But once put into the hands of a skillful potter, it grows rapidly under his fashioning into a vessel he can be proud to claim as his handiwork. In the same way, the soul given over to the working of the heavenly Potter grows rapidly by His Spirit into the image of Jesus.

Once you have taken the step of faith by which you put yourself wholly and absolutely into God's hands, you must expect Him to begin to work. His way of accomplishing what you have entrusted to Him may be different from what you had in mind. But you must rest in the assurance that He knows what He is doing.

Flora entered into this life of faith with a great outpouring of the Spirit and a wonderful flood of light and joy. Thinking that this was a preparation for some great service, she expected to be led at once into a public ministry. Instead, her husband almost immediately suffered a severe business loss, and she had to stay at home and manage a large and busy household. She had no time or energy left for any activities outside of her home. Accepting the discipline, she swept, dusted, baked, and sewed with as much devotion as she would have preached, taught, or written for the Lord. Through this period of training, God was able to make her into a ". . . vessel for noble use . . . ready for any good work" (2 Timothy 2:21 RSV).

Gretchen came into the life of faith under similar circumstances, and she, too, expected to be sent out to do some great work. Instead, she found herself confined at home with two invalid children to care for. Unlike Flora, she complained, fretted, and finally rebelled against her lot in life. As a result, she lost all her joy and became a miserable and bitter woman. She had understood her part of trusting God to begin with, but had not understood God's process of accomplishing that for which she had trusted Him. Because she took herself out of the hands of the heavenly Potter, the vessel was marred on the wheel.

I believe many a vessel has been damaged, many a potential ministry has been lost, through failure to understand God's part in the process of sanctification. A Christian doesn't reach maturity in a moment; but gradually, by the energizing and transforming power of God's Holy Spirit, he is made to "grow up into [Christ] in all things" (Ephesians 4:15). The only way we can hope to reach this maturity is by yielding ourselves willingly and without res-

ervation to His mighty working. The *first step* in santifica-
tion, however, doesn't consist in maturity of growth but in
surrender; and this may be as complete in the newborn
Christian as in the veteran believer.

From the minute the lump of clay comes under the hand
of the potter, it is just what he wants it to be at each stage of
its transformation. Therefore it pleases him, even though
it is far from being the beautiful vase he intends to make it.

A three-month-old infant may be all that a baby could or
should be, and therefore he pleases his mother completely.
But he is far from being what his mother will want him to
be when he reaches manhood.

The green apple of June may be a perfect apple for
June—the best apple that June can produce. But it is
very different from the ripe, red apple of October. God's
works are perfect in every stage of their growth. Man's
works are never perfect until they are complete in every
detail.

Once again, then, let us review our part in the process of
sanctification. First, we must take the *step of faith* by which
we put ourselves into the hands of the Lord, trusting Him
to work in us all the "good pleasure of his will" (Ephesians
1:5). Then, by a *continuous exercise of faith,* we must keep
ourselves there. Don't think that trusting God once for
salvation is all there is to it. Trust is not only the beginning of the Christian life; it is also its continuing foundation. When we trust, the Lord works; and His work is the
important part of the matter. When we do our part, He
never fails to do His.

A saw can accomplish its work of sawing a board in two
only if it is yielded to the hand of the carpenter. The saw is
the instrument used; the power that uses it is the carpen-

ter's. In the same way, when we yield ourselves to God, we find that He works in us to make us "willing and able to obey his own purpose" (Philippians 2:13 TEV). Then we can say with Paul, "I laboured . . . yet not I, but the grace of God which was with me" (1 Corinthians 15:10).

A part of God's divine plan is that His working is dependent upon our cooperation. Our Lord could "do no mighty work" (Mark 6:5) among the Nazarenes because of their unbelief. Mark doesn't say that He *would* not, but that He *could* not. We often think that God *will* not do something for us or in us, when the truth is that He *can*not. Not even the most skillful potter can make a beautiful vessel out of clay that is never put into his hands, and not even God can make me a vessel unto His honor unless I put myself into His hands.

This book is mostly about man's side in the life of faith, since I am writing for human beings in the hope of teaching them how to fulfill their part of this life. God's work on His side, however, must be kept constantly in mind. Unless I believed with all my heart that He is able to accomplish that for which we trust Him, not one word of this book would ever have been written.

3

The Life Defined

In chapter one, I tried to make two points clear: (1) the Christian life described in the Scriptures, the life "hid with Christ in God," is one of abiding rest and continual victory—a life very different from the ordinary experience of Christians; (2) the Bible shows us a Savior who is able to save us from the *power* of sin as surely as He saves us from the *penalty* of sin.

In the second chapter the two distinct sides of this life—the part to be done by the Lord and the part we have to do—were discussed in some detail.

Now let us examine this hidden life more closely and see how it differs from ordinary Christian experience. Simply stated, the essence of it is this: letting the Lord carry our burdens and manage our affairs for us, instead of trying to do so ourselves.

Most Christians are like the man who was overtaken by a wagon while he was struggling along the road under the weight of a heavy load. When the driver offered him a ride, he gratefully climbed in and took a seat. Instead of putting down his burden, however, he kept it on his shoulders.

"Why don't you lay down your bundle?" asked the driver.

"Oh, thank you!" replied the man. "But it is almost too much to ask you to carry *me*. I couldn't think of letting you carry my burden too."

Just so, many Christians who have given themselves into Jesus' care and keeping still continue to carry their own burdens, and often remain weary from the load throughout the whole journey of life.

What do I mean by *burdens*? I mean everything that troubles us, whether spiritual or worldly, inward or outward. First of all, I mean *ourselves*.

The greatest burden we have to carry in life, the most difficult thing we have to manage, is self. Our own daily round of existence, our bodies and emotions, our private weaknesses and temptations—our inward concerns of every kind: these are the things that worry us more than anything else. These are the cares that most often rob us of our joy.

In laying down your burdens, therefore, the first one you must get rid of is yourself. You must hand over yourself and all your concerns into the care and keeping of your God, and *leave them there*. He made you; therefore He surely understands you and knows how to manage you, if you will only trust Him to do it.

Say to Him, "Here, Lord, I turn myself over to You. I have tried in every way possible to manage myself and to make myself what I know I ought to be, but I have failed. Now I give the job to You. Please take complete possession of me. Work in me all that You will. Fashion me into a vessel pleasing and useful to You. I leave myself in Your hands, because I believe Your promise that You will make me into a vessel suitable for Your use." Then you must rest in this commitment, trusting Him absolutely.

Next, you must lay aside every other burden you have been carrying: your health, your reputation, your church work, your home, your children, your business, your finances, your associates—*everything* that is a source of anxiety to you.

All Christians commit to the Lord's keeping the matter

of eternal life, because they know for sure that they can't acquire this on their own. Most Christians, however, continue to carry the concerns of the earthly life on their own shoulders. Perhaps they feel that it is enough to ask the Lord to carry *them,* without asking Him to carry their burdens too.

Laura, a Christian friend of mine, once had an unhappy situation in her life that kept her from sleeping, took away her appetite, and came near to ruining her health. One day, when the situation seemed almost unbearable, she came across a little tract called *Hannah's Faith.* It told the story of a woman who had lived a victorious life in spite of having an unusual amount of trouble. A visitor said to her one day, "Hannah, I don't see how you could bear so much sorrow."

"I didn't bear it," was the quick reply. "The Lord bore it for me."

The visitor commented piously, "Yes, we must take our troubles to the Lord."

"We must do more than that," replied Hannah. "We must *leave* them there. Most people take their burdens to Him, but they bring them away with them again and remain worried and unhappy. But when I take mine, I leave them with Him and come away and forget them. If the worry comes back, I take it to Him again. I do this over and over, until at last I reach perfect rest."

Laura was so much impressed by this tract that she decided to try Hannah's method. Since the circumstances of her life couldn't be altered, she handed them over to the Lord. Then, trusting that He had taken charge of the situation, she left all the responsibility and the worry with Him. Whenever her anxieties reappeared, she took them back to Him. As a result, she was kept in perfect peace in the midst of her troubles. She felt that she had discovered a practical secret, and she never again tried to carry her own burdens. Instead, she handed them over, as fast as they arose, to the divine Burden-bearer.

Then Laura began to apply this secret to her inner concerns, which were even more unmanageable than the outward circumstances of her life. She gave her whole self to the Lord—all that she was and all that she had. Believing that He took full responsibility for that which she had committed to Him, she ceased to fret and worry. As a result, her life began to glow with the joy of belonging to Him. At last she was living the Christian life to the fullest.

Laura's life was changed by the discovery of a very simple secret: that it is possible to obey God's command found in Philippians 4:6: "Have no anxiety about anything, but in everything by prayer and supplication with thanksgiving let your requests be made known to God" (RSV). When she obeyed this command, she found the accompanying promise to be true: "And the peace of God, which passes all understanding, will keep your hearts and your minds in Christ Jesus" (Philippians 4:7 RSV).

Much more could be said about this life "hid with Christ in God," and I could give many examples of what Jesus does for those who truly put themselves in His hands. But the gist of the matter is *total commitment* and *total trust*. The person who discovers this secret has found the key that will unlock all of God's treasures.

I hope I have made you hungry for this kind of life. Wouldn't you like to get rid of your burdens? Don't you long to place your unmanageable self in the hands of One who is able to manage you? Aren't you tired? Doesn't the rest I speak of look sweet to you?

Remember the delicious sense of rest you sometimes have when you climb into bed after a day of strenuous exertion. What a delightful sensation to relax every muscle and let the bed take over the work of supporting your weary body! You trust yourself completely to the bed, and it holds you up without effort or even thought on your part. You *rest*.

But suppose you began to doubt the strength or the stability of your bed, and expected each moment to have it give way beneath you and land you on the floor. Could you rest then? More probably, you would strain every muscle in a fruitless effort to hold yourself up, and as a result you would be more exhausted in the morning than when you went to bed.

This analogy teaches what it means to "rest in the Lord" (Psalms 37:7). Trust yourself to His loving care as you trust your body to the bed. Relax, and cast off every burden. Let yourself go, assured that you are perfectly safe since He is holding you up. Your part is simply to rest; His part is to sustain you. And He cannot fail.

Another analogy, used by Jesus Himself, is that of the child's life. "And calling to him a child, he . . . said, '. . . unless you turn and become like children, you will never enter the kingdom of heaven' " (Matthew 18:2, 3 RSV).

What is a little child like? How does he live? He is free from care, because his life is a life of trust. He trusts his parents, his baby-sitters, his teachers. He provides nothing for himself; yet everything is provided. He goes in and out of his father's house with confidence, enjoying all the good things it contains without having spent a penny to buy them. He lives in the present moment and receives his life unquestioningly as it comes to him day by day.

Once I visited a wealthy family which had only one child—an adopted daughter. Upon her were lavished all the love, tenderness, and care that human hearts could bestow. As I watched that child running in and out of the home, lighthearted and carefree, I realized that her life was a wonderful picture of our position as children in the house of our heavenly Father. And I said to myself, "Nothing would sadden this child's adoptive parents more than to see her worried or anxious about herself in any way: about whether her food and clothes would be provided for her, or how she was to get her education. How much more it must wound the great, loving heart of our God and Father to see His children becoming anxious about themselves and their future!" And I understood why our Lord said so emphatically to His disciples, ". . . do not be anxious about your life . . . ." (Matthew 6:25 RSV).

Who is the best cared for in every household? Isn't it the little child? And doesn't the least of all, the helpless baby, receive the largest share of love and attention? The life of faith that I am writing about consists of just this: being a child in the Father's house. If you can become such a child, your weary, burdened life will be transformed into one of blessedness and rest.

Does anything please a parent more than his child's confidence and freedom from care? You are God's child, and you can please Him by leaving yourself in His hands and literally having "no anxiety about anything." Then you, like Laura, will experience "the peace of God, which passes all understanding."

"Thou dost keep him in perfect peace, whose mind is stayed on thee, because he trusts in thee" (Isaiah 26:3 RSV). This is the divine description of the life of faith—the life that is "hid with Christ in God."

4

How to Enter In

At this point you may be wondering how to enter upon this life of full trust. First you must realize that this life cannot be attained; it is *obtained.* We cannot earn it; we cannot climb up to it; we cannot win it; we can do nothing but ask for it and receive it. It is the gift of God in Christ Jesus.

When a person is offered a gift, the only thing he needs to do is to take it and thank the giver. We never say of a gift, "See what I have attained!" and boast of our skill and wisdom in attaining it. Instead, we say, "See what has been given me!" If we boast, we boast of the love and wealth and generosity of the giver.

Everything in our salvation is a gift. From beginning to end, God is the giver, and we are the receivers. The richest promises are made, not to those who do great things, but to those who "receive . . . God's grace, and his gift of righteousness" (Romans 5:17 NEB). Therefore, in order to experience this life of trust, the Christian must have a receptive attitude. He must recognize that this life is to be God's gift in Christ Jesus and that it cannot be gained by any efforts or works of his own. The only two conditions for receiving this gift are (1) complete consecration and (2) faith to receive.

Why is consecration so important? Not because it is a legal requirement for gaining the blessing, but simply because it removes the difficulties in the way of God's bestowing the gift. If a lump of clay is to be made into a beautiful vase, it must be entirely given over to the potter and must lie passive in his hands. If a soul is to be made into a vessel suitable for God's use, it must be entirely given over to Him and must lie passive in His hands. This is obvious.

I was once trying to explain to a physician the meaning and importance of consecration, but he seemed unable to understand. Finally I said to him, "Suppose a patient asked you to take charge of his case but refused to tell you all his symptoms or to take all your prescriptions. He might say to you, 'I am willing to follow your directions when they seem sensible to me; but if they don't, I will use my own judgment.' What would you do in such a case?"

"Do!" was his indignant reply. "I would refuse to accept him as a patient. I could do nothing for him, unless he put his whole case into my hands and obeyed my directions implicitly."

"Then obedience to the doctor's orders is essential if the patient wants to be cured?"

"Absolutely!"

"And that is consecration," I told him. "God must have the whole life put into His hands without any reservations, and His directions must be implicitly followed."

"I see it!" he exclaimed. "I see it, and I'll do it! From now on, I'll let God have His own way with me."

Perhaps the word *abandonment* might express this idea more clearly than *consecration*. In either case, what we mean is an entire surrender of the whole being to God. Spirit, soul, and body must be placed under His absolute control, for Him to do with as He pleases. We must say under all circumstances and in every decision, "Thy will be done." We are to give up all freedom of choice and to lead lives of unquestioning obedience.

To a person who doesn't know God, this self-surrender may look hard. But to those who know Him, it is happiness and rest. He is our Father, and He loves us and knows what is best for us. Therefore His will is the most blessed thing that can come to us under any circumstances. How is it that Satan has succeeded in blinding the eyes of so many

Christians to this fact? God's own children are afraid of His will—His lovely, lovable will, which holds only kindness, mercy, and eternal blessing.

I wish I could show everyone the indescribable sweetness of the will of God. Heaven is a place of bliss, because it is where His will is perfectly done in us. He loves us—*loves us*—and the will of love is always blessing for its loved one. You who know what it is to love know that, if you had your way, your loved ones would be overwhelmed with blessings. All that is good and sweet and lovely in life would be poured out upon them.

If this is the way of love with us, how much more must it be so with our God, who is Love itself! If only we could have a glimpse into the depths of His love, we would rush out to embrace His will as our richest treasure. We would joyfully hand ourselves over to Him, grateful that such a privilege can be ours.

Yet many Christians actually seem to think that God is just waiting for a chance to make them miserable and to take away all their joy. They imagine—poor souls!—that they can stop Him from doing this by sheer determination to hold on to all the temporal gifts He has given them. Hundreds of lives are being made wretched by this attitude.

My friend Sue once felt this way. Finally she confessed to me that she was actually afraid to say, "Thy will be done." Sue had one child—a little boy whom she dearly loved. I said to her, "Suppose your little Charlie should come to you and say, 'Mother, I have decided to do everything you want me to from now on. I am always going to

obey you, and I want you to do whatever you think is best
for me. I know you love me, and I will trust your love.'

"How would you feel toward him? Would you say to
yourself, 'Ah, now I have a chance to make Charlie miserable! I will take away all his pleasures and fill his life with
every hard and disagreeable chore I can find. I will compel
him to do the very tasks that are most difficult for him and
will give him all sorts of impossible commands'?"

"Oh, no!" exclaimed Sue indignantly. "You know I
wouldn't! I would be more eager than ever to fill his life
with good things."

"And are *you* more tender and loving than God?" I
asked.

Sue got the message. "I see my mistake," she said. "From
now on I won't be afraid of saying, 'Thy will be done' to my
heavenly Father, any more than I would want Charlie to be
afraid of saying it to me."

The will of our God is better than health, friends,
money, fame, ease, or prosperity. It brightens our darkest
hours and sheds light on the gloomiest paths. If you have
made God's will your kingdom, you will always reign in
confidence. Surely, then, you can see that it is a privilege to
take the first step into the life "hid with Christ in God"—
the step of total consecration. I hope you don't regard it as
a hard and stern demand. You must do it gladly, thankfully, enthusiastically. Look on consecration as a *privilege,*
and I can assure you from my own experience that you will
find in it the greatest happiness you have ever known.

Faith is the other condition for experiencing this higher
Christian life. Faith is absolutely essential to receiving any
gift. No matter how freely a friend gives you a present, it is
not really yours until you *believe* it has been given to you

and claim it as your own. This is especially true of intangible gifts. Your husband or your wife may love you above all else in this world; but unless you believe in that love, your life remains loveless.

Most Christians seem to understand this principle with regard to forgiveness. They know that Jesus died so that their sins might be forgiven. They also know that forgiveness did not become theirs until they believed this doctrine and accepted God's forgiveness. When it comes to living the Christian life, however, they seem to lose sight of this principle. Having been saved by faith, they think that they are now to live by works and efforts; that instead of continuing to *receive,* they are now to begin to *do.*

Such Christians are completely unable to grasp the truth that the "life hid with Christ in God" is also experienced by faith. Yet Scripture plainly states that *as* we have received Christ Jesus the Lord, *so* we are to walk in Him (Colossians 2:6). We received Him by faith alone; therefore we are to walk in Him by faith alone. And the faith by which we enter into this hidden life is just the same as the faith by which we were brought out of the kingdom of Satan into the Kingdom of God.

First, we believed that Jesus saved us from the guilt of our sin—and we were freed from guilt by faith. *Now,* we must believe that He saves us from the *power* of sin, and sin will lose its power over us. *First,* we trusted Him for our forgiveness, and it became ours. *Now,* we must trust Him for our sanctification, and it will become ours also. *First,* we took Him as a Savior from the penalties of our sins in the future. *Now,* we must take Him as a Savior from our bondage to sin in the present. *First,* He was our Savior; *now,* He is to be our Life. *First,* He lifted us out of the pit;

now, He wants to set us in "heavenly places" with Himself (Ephesians 2:6).

All that I have been saying is to be experienced in everyday living. Theoretically, according to Scripture, every believer is given everything the minute he is converted. But in experience, nothing is his until he claims it by faith. God ". . . has bestowed on us in Christ every spiritual blessing in the heavenly realms" (Ephesians 1:3 NEB). Until we receive these blessings by faith, however, they do not become ours in practical experience. "According to your faith" (Matthew 9:29) always defines and limits what we actually experience.

The faith of which I am speaking must be *today's* faith. No faith that is exercised in the future tense amounts to anything. A man may believe forever that his sins *will be* forgiven at some future time, but this belief is not the belief of conversion. He has to come to the *now* belief and say by faith, "I know my sins are now forgiven," before he can be born again.

By the same token, no faith which looks for a future deliverance from the *power* of sin will ever lead a soul into the life I have been describing. Satan delights in this "future faith," for he knows it cannot accomplish anything. But he trembles and flees when the believer dares to claim an immediate deliverance, and to regard himself as free from his power *right now.*

Let me sum it up for you. In order to enter into this life of rest and triumph, you have two steps to take: entire consecration, or abandonment, and absolute faith. No matter what your circumstances may be, no matter what

your difficulties, your surroundings, or your associates—if
you take these two steps and persevere in them, they will
certainly bring you out sooner or later into the green pastures and still waters of this higher Christian walk. *You may
be sure of this!* Forget everything else and simply concentrate on these two points. If you take these two steps and
are very clear and definite about having done so, your
progess will be rapid, and you will reach your goal far
sooner than you expect.

Shall I go through it all once more, so that there will be
no misunderstanding?

You are a child of God and want very much to please
Him. You love Jesus, your Savior, and are sick and tired of
the sin that grieves Him. You long to be free from its
power. Everything you have tried up to this point has
failed to set you free, and you are getting desperate. Is it
really true, as some Christians claim, that Jesus is able and
willing to free you *now?*

Surely, deep down in your heart, you know that He is!
In fact, the very thing He came to do was to save you from
all your enemies. Then trust Him! Commit your life to
Him in absolute abandonment, and believe that He takes
it. Then, knowing who He is and what He has promised,
claim right now that He *fully* saves you.

Just as you believed at first that He delivered you from
the guilt of sin because He promised it, believe now that
He delivers you from the power of sin, because He promised it. Let your faith now lay hold of a new power in
Christ. You have trusted Him as your dying Savior; now
trust Him as your *living* Savior, who comes to deliver you
from your present bondage just as much as He came to
deliver you from future punishment. You are just as pow-

erless to do one as to do the other. You can no more sanctify yourself than you could have forgiven your own sins. Jesus, and Jesus only, must do both for you. Your part in both cases is simply to give the thing to Him to do, and then believe that He does it.

A woman who is now very mature in this life of trust found it hard to enter in. She said to the friend who was counseling her, "You say, 'Let go and trust; let go and trust.' But I don't know *how*. I wish you would just do it out loud, so that I can see how you do it."

Let me do it "out loud" for you:

Lord Jesus, I believe that You are able and willing to deliver me from all the care and anxiety and bondage of my present life. I believe You died to set me free, not only in the future, but here and now. I believe You are stronger than Satan, and that You can keep me—even me, weak as I am—from falling into his snares.

And, Lord, I'm going to *trust* You to keep me. I've tried keeping myself and have failed completely. I am absolutely helpless. So now I give myself to You—body, soul, and spirit. I keep back nothing. Take me and make me into anything Your love and Your wisdom shall choose.

And now, I *am* Yours. I believe You have taken possession of my heart and have already begun to work in me. I trust You completely, and I trust You *now*.

Are you afraid to take this step? Does it seem too sudden, too much like a leap in the dark? Don't you know that the steps of faith always seem like steps into a void? But underneath is the rock. If ever you are to enter this abundant life, you must sooner or later take these first steps of consecration and trust, for there is no other way. To do it now may save you months or years of disappointment and grief. Hear the word of the Lord: "This is my command: be strong, be resolute; do not be fearful or dismayed, for the Lord your God is with you wherever you go" (Joshua 1:9 NEB).

5

Difficulties Concerning Consecration

I must warn you that Satan uses many devices to oppose every step of the Christian's progress. He is especially busy when he sees a believer becoming hungry and thirsty for a closer relationship with God, and reaching out to receive all that Jesus has for him.

One of Satan's tricks is to make you doubt your consecration. As soon as you try to consecrate yourself in order to enter the life "hid with Christ in God," you meet with difficulty. You think you have consecrated yourself, and yet you feel no different; nothing seems changed. Completely baffled, you ask, "How am I to *know* when I have taken the step of consecration?"

At this point Satan never fails to employ one of his most successful diversions: that of turning your attention to *feelings*. Many Christians, unfortunately, put feeling first and faith second. If you are such a person and do not *feel* consecrated, it is impossible for you to believe that God has taken charge of your life.

God's rule in everything is *faith first and feeling second*. When Satan tries to make you doubt your consecration, simply follow God's rule and put faith before feeling. Give yourself to the Lord as definitely and fully as you know how, and ask the Holy Spirit to show you anything in your heart or your life that is not pleasing to Him. If He shows you anything, give it to the Lord immediately and say, "Thy will be done." If He shows you nothing, then you must believe that there is nothing, that you have given Him all. Then you must *believe* that He has taken over. You positively must not wait to *feel*, either that you have given yourself or that God has accepted you. You must simply believe that it has been done, and act on that belief.

When a man proposes to a young lady, he is offering his

lifelong love and loyalty to her and asking her to accept them. Since these are not material gifts, the transaction is entirely one of faith. Now suppose a man proposed marriage to a young lady and she accepted him. Then suppose that, after he went away, he began to wonder whether he had actually asked her to marry him and she had actually said yes. If he became really doubtful, he might go back the next day and propose again, and perhaps she would be understanding enough to accept him again. If this happened every day for a period of weeks, however, both of them would surely begin to doubt his intention to give her his love for life.

Is this the way you have been acting toward God in the matter of consecration? Have you given yourself to Him over and over—perhaps every day for months—and yet are still wondering whether you have *really* given yourself after all, and whether He has *really* taken you? Are you about to conclude, because you don't *feel* any different, that the transaction has not been made?

Let me warn you that this sort of perplexity will last forever, unless you cut it short by faith! You must come to the point of looking on your consecration and its acceptance by God as accomplished facts before you can possibly expect any change of feeling.

The law of offerings to the Lord, stated in Leviticus 27:28, makes it plain that everything given to God becomes something holy *by that very act of dedication*. Once given, it cannot, without sacrilege, be put to any other use.

> . . . nothing which a man devotes to the Lord irredeemably from his own property, whether man or beast or ancestral land, may be sold or

redeemed. Everything so devoted is most holy to
the Lord.

NEB

The Israelite might have made his offering grudgingly
or halfheartedly; but once he had made it, the matter was
taken out of his hands and the offering, by God's own law,
became "holy to the Lord." It was not the intention of the
giver that made it holy, but the holiness of the receiver.
Our Lord Himself said that "the altar sanctifies the gift"
(*see* Matthew 23:19 PHILLIPS). Once laid upon the altar, an
offering from that moment belongs to the Lord.

I can imagine an Israelite who had deposited a gift on
the altar beginning to search his heart as to his motives,
and then coming back to the priest to say that he was afraid
he had not been perfectly sincere in giving it. I feel sure
that the priest would have silenced him at once, saying, "I
am not concerned about your motives in giving your offering. The fact is that you *did* give it, and now it is the
Lord's, for 'everything so devoted is most holy' to Him. It
is too late now to recall the transaction!" The priest, and all
Israel, would have been aghast if the man had reached out
to take back his offering.

It is sad to think that earnest Christians are guilty of a
similar sacrilege. Having given themselves to the Lord in
solemn consecration, they take back, through unbelief,
that which they have laid on the altar.

The fact that God is not visibly present makes it difficult
to believe in the reality of a transaction made with Him. If
we could actually see Him present with us when we make
our acts of consecration, it would be easier for us to realize
that we have given Him our word. Then we would not

dare to take it back, no matter how much we might want to. The transaction would seem as binding to us as a spoken promise made to an earthly friend.

We need to realize that God's presence is always a certain fact, and that our every act is done right before Him. A word spoken in prayer is spoken to Him just as surely as if our eyes could see Him and our hands could touch Him. Once we realize this, our relation with Him will no longer seem so vague, and we will feel the binding force of every word we say in His presence.

Perhaps you are thinking, "If He would only speak to me and say that He took me when I gave myself to Him, I would have no trouble believing it." Of course you wouldn't! But He doesn't as a rule give us this assurance until we first believe what He has already promised in His Word.

By commanding us to present ourselves to Him as "a living sacrifice" (Romans 12:1), He has pledged Himself to receive us. No honorable man would ask another to give him something that he wasn't sure he would accept. Still less would a loving parent act in this way toward a child. When we surrender ourselves to the Lord according to His own command, we may feel completely confident that He receives us then and there. From that moment on, we are His. A real transaction has taken place—one which we know will not be voided by Him, and which cannot be voided by us without dishonor.

Deuteronomy 26:17–19 tells us how God works in such a situation:

> You have declared this day concerning the
> Lord that he is your God, and that you will walk

> in his ways, and keep his statutes and his com-
> mandments and his ordinances, and will obey his
> voice; and the Lord has declared this day con-
> cerning you that you are a people for his own
> possession, as he has promised you, and that you
> are to keep all his commandments . . . and that
> you shall be a people holy to the Lord your God,
> as he has spoken.
>
> RSV

When we declare that the Lord is our God and that we
will walk in His ways and keep His commandments, He
declares that we are His and that we *are* to keep all His
commandments. From that moment He takes possession
of us. This has always been His way of working, and it
always will be. "Everything so devoted is most holy to the
Lord." What could be plainer?

If this promise from the Old Testament hasn't settled all
your doubts, there is a New Testament declaration which is
equally positive, although it approaches the subject from a
different angle. It is found in 1 John 5:14, 15:

> And this is the confidence which we have in
> him, that if we ask anything according to his will
> he hears us. And if we know that he hears us in
> whatever we ask, we know that we have obtained
> the requests made of him.
>
> RSV

Is it according to His will that you should be entirely
consecrated to Him? Of course it is, for He has commanded it (Matthew 10:37–39). Isn't it also according to

His will that He should work ". . . in you, inspiring both
the will and the deed, for his own chosen purpose"
(Philippians 2:13 NEB)? Again, the answer is obvious. Since
you know, then, that these things *are* according to God's
will, you have His own word that He hears you when you
ask for them. Further, you have His word that you have
obtained the requests you have made of Him.

That you *have* obtained, the Scripture says—not that you
will obtain or *may* obtain—but that you have *already* obtained. This is the sort of present faith by which we receive
what God has promised (Hebrews 11:33) and which gives
us access to the grace that is ours in Jesus Christ (Romans
5:2). By this *present* faith our hearts are purified like those
of Cornelius and the members of his household (Acts
15:9), and we are enabled to live, stand, and walk by faith.

In order to make this matter so plain and practical that
no one will have any further difficulty with it, I will repeat
again just what you must do to end forever your doubts
about your consecration.

I am assuming that you have trusted Jesus for the forgiveness of your sins and that, through faith in Him, you
have been made a member of God's family (Galatians
3:26). And now you long to become like Jesus. You know
that this can be done only if you surrender yourself to Him
completely, so that He can have His way in your life. You
have tried over and over to make this surrender, but apparently without success. Let me tell you what you must do
now.

Come to Him once more and surrender your whole self
to His will, as completely as you know how. Ask Him to
reveal to you by His Spirit any hidden rebellion. If He
shows you nothing, then you must believe that there *is*

nothing, and that the surrender is complete. Then consider the matter settled. You have abandoned yourself to the Lord, and you no longer belong to yourself. You must not listen to Satan's suggestions to the contrary.

If the temptation comes to wonder whether you really have made a complete surrender, affirm again that you *have*. Don't argue the matter. Repel the suggestion instantly and emphatically. You meant it then; you mean it now; you have really done it. Your feelings may fight against the surrender, but your will must hold firm. It is your *purpose* God looks at—not how you feel about that purpose. Therefore the only thing you need be certain about is your purpose, or will.

Now the surrender has been made, never to be questioned or recalled. The next step is to believe that God takes what you have surrendered to Him and to regard it as His—right now. You must believe that He has begun to work in you, "inspiring both the will and the deed, for his own chosen purpose."

And *here you must rest*. There is nothing more for you to do. You are the Lord's now—absolutely and entirely in His hands. He has undertaken the whole care and management and forming of you and will, according to His Word, ". . . make of [you] what he would have [you] be through Jesus Christ . . ." (Hebrews 13:21 NEB). But you must hold steady here. If you begin to question your surrender or God's acceptance of it, your wavering faith will produce a wavering experience, and He cannot work. *While you trust, He works.* And the result of His working is that you are changed, by degrees, into the likeness of Christ (2 Corinthians 3:18).

6
Difficulties Concerning Faith

After consecration, the next step in the believer's progress out of the wilderness into the promised land of the life "hid with Christ in God" is the step of *faith*. Here again, Satan is skillful in putting obstacles in the way.

By now, you are fully aware that this higher Christian life for which you are longing can be received only by faith. But faith itself is a mystery to many Christians. If you are one of these, you may be confused and discouraged rather than helped when someone tells you that faith is an essential requirement for entering this life.

"I know it has to be by faith," you say; "for I know that everything in the Christian life is by faith. That is what makes it so hard—because I *have* no faith. I don't even know what it is, or how to get it!" And this difficulty about faith may lead you close to despair.

If this is your problem, you are not alone; for the subject of faith is often misunderstood. Actually, faith is the simplest and plainest thing in the world.

Most people think of faith as either a religious exercise of the soul or an attitude of the heart—something that can be used as a passport to God's favor or as a coin with which to purchase His gifts. If you have been praying for faith with this concept in mind, it is no wonder that you have never received an answer to your prayer and are convinced that you have no faith.

Faith is nothing of this sort. It is not a possession. It is simply *believing God*. Like sight, faith is nothing apart from its object. Looking inside to discover whether you have faith is like shutting your eyes and looking inside to see whether you have sight. You know that you have sight when you see something; you know that you have faith when you believe something. Just as sight is only seeing, faith is only believing.

The essential thing about seeing is that you see the thing as it is; the essential thing about believing is that you believe the thing as it is. The virtue lies not in your believing, but in *what* you believe. If you believe the truth, you are saved; if you believe a lie, you are lost. The act of believing is the same in both cases; it is the thing believed that makes the all-important difference. Your salvation comes, not from your belief, but from the Savior in whom you believe. Your believing is nothing but the link.

Please recognize the extreme simplicity of faith! It is so simple that it is hard to explain. Faith is nothing more or less than just believing God. When He says in His Word that He has done something for us, or that He will do it, *trust* Him to do it!

What does it mean to trust someone to do a piece of work for you? It means letting that person do it, and feeling no need to do it yourself. Every one of us has trusted very important tasks to other people in this way. If we had confidence in those people, we felt perfectly ,afe in doing so. Mothers trust their precious babies to the care of relatives or baby-sitters without any great anxiety. All of us trust our health and our lives every day to cooks, bus drivers, mechanics, and all sorts of workmen who could kill us or ruin our lives in an instant, either deliberately or by a moment's carelessness. We never feel that we are doing anything in the least remarkable when we put ourselves at the mercy of people whom we know only slightly, if at all.

You yourself could not live on this earth and go through the routine of a single day if you couldn't trust your fellow men. It never enters your head to say you cannot. Yet you do not hesitate to say, continually, that you cannot trust your God!

Try now to imagine yourself acting in your human relationships as you do in your relationship with God. Suppose you should begin tomorrow with the notion that you couldn't trust anybody, because you had no faith. When you sat down to breakfast, you would say, "I can't eat anything on this table, because I have no faith. I can't believe that my wife hasn't put poison in the coffee, or that the sausage has been properly processed and cooked." So you would leave the table hungry. Then when you started to work, you would say, "I can't take the car, because I have no faith. I can't trust the engineer who designed it, the workers who made, inspected, and assembled the parts, or the mechanic who serviced it." So you would be compelled to walk to work and everywhere else you wanted to go.

Then when your friends told you about something that had happened to a mutual acquaintance, you would say, "I'm so sorry that I can't believe you; but I have no faith, and never can believe anybody." When a customer wanted to open a charge account, you would tell him, "I'm sorry, but I can't trust you. I have no faith in anybody." If you tried to read a newspaper, you would soon lay it down again, saying, "I can't believe a word this paper says, for I have no faith. I don't believe there is any such person as the president, for I never saw him, or any such country as Ireland, for I was never there. Since I have no faith, I can't believe anything that I haven't actually felt and touched myself. It's a great trial, but I can't do anything about it, because I have no faith."

Just imagine how disastrous such a day would be and how foolish you would appear to anyone observing you.

Your friends would be insulted, and your customers would take their business elsewhere! Now ask yourself how God must feel when you tell Him that You cannot trust Him or believe His Word because you have no faith.

How is it possible that you can trust your fellow men and cannot trust your God? You can receive the "testimony of men" and cannot receive the "testimony of God" (*see* 1 John 5:9 RSV)? You can believe man's records and cannot believe God's records? You can commit your dearest earthly interests to fallible human beings, yet are afraid to commit your spiritual interests to Jesus, who gave His life for the very purpose of saving you and who is able to save you "fully and completely" (*see* Hebrews 7:25 PHILLIPS)?

If you call yourself a believer, surely you will never again dare to plead that you have no faith. For when you say this, you are saying that you have no faith in God. You are not asked to have faith in yourself; in fact, you would be in a sorry state if you did have. The next time you say, "I have no faith" or "I can't believe," remember to complete the sentence and say, "I have no faith in *God;* I can't believe *God.*" Surely then you will overcome this bad habit!

Perhaps you now say, "But I can't believe without the Holy Spirit." Are you blaming your lack of faith on the Spirit's failure to do His work? If so, you are still making God a liar (1 John 5:10), for He says in His Word that the Holy Spirit ". . . helps us in our weakness . . ." (Romans 8:26 RSV). We never have to wait for Him; He is always waiting for us and is always ready to do His work. Your failure to believe is not the Spirit's fault, but your own.

Put your will, then, over onto the believing side. Say, "Lord, I will believe; I *do* believe," and continue to say it.

Insist upon believing, no matter how many doubts Satan may raise. Put reckless confidence in the Word and promises of God, and have the courage to abandon yourself to the keeping and saving power of Jesus. If you have ever entrusted an important matter to any earthly friend, entrust yourself and all your spiritual interests *now* to your heavenly Friend, and never, *never*, NEVER allow yourself to doubt again.

If there are any two things more utterly incompatible than oil and water, they are *trust* and *worry*. Would you call it trust if you asked a friend to do something for you, and then spent your time worrying about whether the matter would be properly handled? And can you call it trust, when you have given to the Lord the saving and keeping of your soul, and are still spending day after day, night after night in anxiety and doubt? When a person *really* trusts a matter to someone else, he ceases to worry about it. If he continues to worry, it is clear that he doesn't trust.

Tested by this rule, how little real trust there is in the church of Christ! No wonder our Lord asked the disquieting question, ". . . When the Son of man comes, will he find faith on earth?" (Luke 18:8 RSV). He will find plenty of work, a great deal of earnestness, and doubtless many devoted hearts; but will He find faith? It is a solemn question, and I hope every Christian will ponder it well. Too long the church has shared in the unbelief of the world! Now let every person who knows the Lord, and believes Him to be trustworthy, demonstrate this belief by trusting Him totally.

Very early in my Christian life, I was deeply stirred by something I read in a volume of old sermons. It was an appeal to all who love the Lord Jesus to let their unwavering faith in Him show others how worthy He is of being trusted. I actually begged God to let me experience trials that would allow me to demonstrate total trust.

It may be that ". . . you have not passed this way before . . ." (Joshua 3:4 RSV), but today you can display your confidence in Jesus by starting out on a life and walk of faith, lived moment by moment in absolute and childlike trust in Him.

You have trusted Him in a few things, and He has not failed you. Trust Him now for everything, and see if He does not do for you immeasurably more than you could ever have asked or thought (Ephesians 3:20 NEB)—not according to *your* power or ability, but according to *His* mighty power.

You don't find it difficult to trust the Lord with the management of the universe. Can your situation be so complex that you need to be anxious about His management of *you?* Put such conceited ideas out of your mind! Take your stand on the power and trustworthiness of your God, and see how quickly all doubts will vanish before a steadfast determination to believe. Trust God in the dark and in the light; trust Him at night and in the morning. Although such faith may require a great effort to begin with, it will sooner or later become easy, natural, and habitual.

❦❧

We have the word of Jesus that ". . . all things are possible with God" (Mark 10:27 RSV) and that ". . . all things are possible to him who believes" (Mark 9:23 RSV). In times past, faith has ". . . subdued kingdoms, wrought righteousness, obtained promises, stopped the mouths of lions, quenched the violence of fire . . . turned to flight the armies of the aliens" (Hebrews 11:33, 34)—and faith can do it again. For our Lord Himself has told us, ". . . If you have faith as a grain of mustard seed, you will say to this mountain, 'Move from here to there,' and it will move; and nothing will be impossible to you" (Matthew 17:20 rsv).

Every child of God should have at least as much faith as a grain of mustard seed. Therefore, do not dare to say again that you can't trust because you have no faith. Say rather, "I can trust my God, and I *will* trust Him. Not all the powers of earth or hell shall be able to make me doubt the faithfulness of my Redeemer!" Of all the forms of worship we can bring Him, none is so sweet to Him as such total, reckless trust.

Then let your faith confirm all God's promises, and believe in Him to see you through every trial. Remember that ". . . even though now you smart for a little while, if need be, under trials of many kinds . . . . these trials come so that your faith may prove itself worthy of all praise, glory, and honour when Jesus Christ is revealed" (1 Peter 1:6, 7 neb).

7

Difficulties Concerning the Will

Now that you have, by consecration and faith, stepped out of yourself into Christ, you should be experiencing something of the joy of the life "hid with Christ in God." But I must warn you about another difficulty that you may have to face.

The feelings of peace and rest that usually—though not always—accompany this step will sooner or later subside. Then you may begin to think that there is no reality in the experience you have had and the decision you have made. You may feel like a hypocrite when you say or even *think* they are real. Perhaps it seems to you that your belief doesn't go below the surface; that it is only *lip* belief, and that your surrender cannot be acceptable to God because it is not a surrender of the heart. You are reluctant to say that you belong entirely to the Lord, for fear you will be telling a lie; yet you cannot bring yourself to say you don't belong to Him, because you so much *want* to be His.

This difficulty is real and may be very discouraging. It can be easily overcome, however, once you thoroughly understand the principle of the new life and have learned *how* to live in it.

Your mistake has been in thinking—as most people do—that the life "hid with Christ in God" is lived in the emotions. Consequently, you have directed all your attention to the way you feel. If your emotional state is satisfactory, you are confident that you are on the right track; if it is unsatisfactory, you are troubled.

The truth of the matter is that this life is not to be lived in the emotions at all, but in the *will*. The reality of the life isn't at all dependent upon your emotional state, but depends entirely upon your keeping *your* will in the center of *God's* will. This is what Fenelon meant when he said that "pure religion resides in the will alone." The will is the power that governs man's nature. If your will is set in the right direction, all the rest of your nature must come into line.

What do I mean when I speak of your *will*? I do not mean your wish or even your purpose, but your choice—the deciding power which everything in you must obey. In short, it is the *ego*—the "real" you.

Some people feel that they are ruled by their emotions. But most of us know from practical experience that there is something deeper within us—something independent of our emotions and our wishes—that makes the final decisions. Our emotions *belong* to us; they are suffered and enjoyed by us, but they are not ourselves. If God is to take possession of us, He must begin by gaining control of the central will. If the Holy Spirit is reigning there, all the rest of our nature must come under His control.

What does all this have to do with the difficulty I am talking about? It has a great deal to do with it. The decisions of our *will* are often directly opposed to the desires of our *emotions*. Therefore, if you are in the habit of considering your emotions as the test, you will probably feel like a hypocrite when you claim the reality of a decision made by the will alone. But as soon as you realize that your will is the power that governs your nature, you can ignore anything that tries to deny the reality of its decisions.

I know this is hard to understand; but it is extremely important to anyone entering into the life of faith. Let me tell you a true story to illustrate what I am trying to say.

A highly intelligent young man—let's call him Robert—was seeking to enter into this new life. He became discouraged when he found himself unable to break his lifelong habit of doubting. To his emotions, nothing seemed real—and the more he struggled, the more unreal it all seemed. I told him this secret about the will that I have just been sharing with you, and urged him to put his will over on to the believing side, to *choose* to believe, to say, deep within himself, "I will believe! I do believe!"

"If you do this," I told him, "you can forget about your emotions. Sooner or later they will come into harmony with your belief."

"Are you telling me that I can *choose* to believe in that way, when nothing seems true to me?" he asked. "Will that kind of believing be *real?*"

"Yes, indeed. Your part is just to put your *will* over on God's side in this matter of believing. When you do this, God takes control of it and works in you to do His will. You will soon find that he has brought all the rest of your nature into subjection to Himself."

"Well," Robert replied, "I can *do* this. I can't control my emotions, but I *can* control my will. If that is all that needs to be done, the new life may be possible for me after all. I can give my will to God, and I *do!*"

From that moment on, Robert held steadily to the decision of his will. His emotions continued to accuse him of being a hypocrite, but he answered them with the assertion that he *chose* to believe, he *meant* to believe, and he *did* believe. After a few days the battle was won, and every emotion, as well as every thought, had been brought "into captivity . . . to the obedience of Christ" (2 Corinthians 10:5), whose Spirit had taken possession of the will that had been put into His hands.

Robert had held fast the *profession* of his faith (Hebrews 4:14) without wavering, even though it had seemed to him at times that he had no real faith to "hold fast." There had been times when it had taken all the willpower he possessed to make his lips *say* that he believed. But he had caught the idea that his will was really *himself;* and that if he kept that on God's side, he was doing all he could do. Then it was up to God to change his emotions and control his being. The result has been one of the most effective Christian lives I know of: simple, direct, and powerful.

Here is where the secret lies. Your will, which is the key to all your actions, has in the past been under the control of Satan, and he has been using it to make your life miserable. Now God says, "Yield yourself up to Me, as one who has 'been brought from death to life' (*see* Romans 6:13 RSV), and I will work in you to inspire 'both the will and the deed, for [My] own chosen purpose' (*see* Philippians 2:13 NEB)." And the moment we yield our wills to Him, He does begin to work in us, giving us the mind of Christ (1 Corinthians 2:16) and shaping us into His likeness (Romans 8:29 NEB).

Perhaps another illustration would be helpful.

Betty had a bad habit which her emotions enjoyed but her will hated. As long as she believed that she was under the control of her emotions, she was unable to conquer it. When she learned this secret about the will, she began to pray in this way:

"Lord, You know that with one part of my nature I love this sin; but in my real, central self I hate it. Now I put my will over on Your side in the matter. I *will* not to do it any more, and I trust You to deliver me from it."

God immediately took possession of Betty's surrendered will and began to work in her. The result was that His will gained the mastery over her emotions, and she found herself delivered from her sinful habit by the power of the Holy Spirit.

Now let me tell you how to apply this secret in your own life. Stop giving any thought to your emotions, for they are only the servants. Just pay attention to your will, which is the real master in your being. Is your *will* given up to God? Has it been put into His hands? Does your will decide to believe? Does your will choose to obey? If so, then *you* are in the Lord's hands, and *you* have decided to believe and have chosen to obey—for your will is yourself.

And now *know* that the thing is done, no matter what your feelings tell you. The transaction with God is just as real when it is done in the will alone as it is when every emotion is in agreement. It doesn't *seem* as real to you; but in God's sight it *is* real. When you have learned the secret that you can ignore your emotions as long as you are sure your *will* is given over to God, all the scriptural commands become possible to you. You are able to yield yourself to God (Romans 6:13), to present your body a "living sacrifice" to Him (Romans 12:1), to abide in Christ (John 15:4, 6, 7; 1 John 2:28), to "walk in the light" (1 John 1:7). You know that your will can take God's side in all these matters, no matter how much your emotions may rebel.

Then don't be troubled by any feeling of unreality or hypocrisy that comes when you submit your will to God. Such feelings stem from your emotions, and therefore can be ignored. Just see to it that your will is in God's hands, that your real self is given over to His working. Place your choice—your decision—on His side, and leave it there.

Your surging emotions are like a boat in the ocean, which is attached by a cable to a safe harbor. Though it may be tossed by the waves, it can be brought into calm water by a steady pull on the cable. In the same way your emotions, finding themselves attached to the mighty power of God by the choice of your will, must inevitably come into the safe harbor of His will and give their allegiance to Him.

The will is like the wise mother of obstreperous children (the emotions). She decides on a course of action that she believes to be right. The children raise a row and say they won't have it; but the mother, knowing that she is in charge, goes calmly ahead with her plans and pays no attention to the uproar. The result is that, sooner or later, the children yield to their mother's authority and go along with her decision—and peace is restored.

If that mother should for a moment entertain the notion that the children were in authority, confusion would reign. Unfortunately, this is just the situation that prevails in some homes—and in many lives where the feelings are allowed to govern instead of the will.

Remember, then, that reality for you is what your *will* decides, and not the verdict of your emotions. You are far more likely to be hypocritical when you allow your actions to be controlled by your feelings than when you hold fast to the decision of your will. If your will is on God's side, there is no hypocrisy in claiming *now* that you belong to Him totally, even though your emotions may deny it.

I am convinced that the word *heart*, as used in the Bible, doesn't refer to the emotions (which is what we now understand the word to mean), but to the will, the central self. The object of God's dealings with man is that this "I" may be yielded up to Him, and this central life given over entirely to His control. It isn't the *feelings* of the man that God wants, but the man himself.

Have you given Him your *self*? Have you yielded your

will to His working? Do you surrender the very center of your being into His hands? Then, regardless of what your emotions tell you, it is your present right to say with the apostle: "I have been crucified with Christ: the life I now live is not my life, but the life which Christ lives in me; and my present bodily life is lived by faith in the Son of God, who loved me and gave himself up for me" (Galatians 2:20 NEB).

After this chapter had been completed, I received a copy of the following letter, written many years ago by one minister to another. It is such a remarkable illustration of the teaching I have tried to present.

> Dear Brother:
>
> I will take a few minutes of the time I have devoted to God to write a note to you, His servant. It is good to feel that we belong entirely to the Lord—that He has received us and called us His. This is what it means to be a Christian: to give up forever the idea that we belong to ourselves and to subscribe fully to Paul's sentiment that we are not our own; we were bought with a price (1 Corinthians 6:19, 20).
>
> Nothing remarkable has happened to me since I saw you. In fact, I don't know that we should look for remarkable things in our Christian experience. We should just keep on trying to be holy, as God is holy.
>
> I don't feel qualified to teach you, but I will be glad to tell you how I have been led. Since the Lord deals differently with every person, we shouldn't try to copy the experience of others. There are some things, however, that have to be

done by everyone who is seeking to be made holy.

First of all, we must make a personal commitment of everything to God—a promise that we will be completely His forever. I made this commitment intellectually, without any change in my feelings. My heart was still hard and full of darkness, unbelief, and sin.

Nevertheless, I promised to be the Lord's and, to the best of my ability, laid myself and everything I am and have on the altar, a living sacrifice. When I rose from my knees, I was painfully conscious that there was no change in my feelings. Yet I was sure that I had, as sincerely and honestly as I was able, committed myself totally and permanently to God. I knew that the work was by no means complete, but I was determined to remain entirely devoted to God—a living, perpetual sacrifice. And now came the effort to do this.

I knew I had to believe that God did accept me and did come to live in my heart. Since I did *not* believe this—much as I wanted to—I prayerfully read the first letter of John in an effort to convince myself that God loves me as an individual.

I was aware that my heart was full of sin. I seemed to be unable to overcome pride or to repel the evil thoughts that I hated. But John says that Christ came to earth "to destroy the works of the devil" (1 John 3:8), and it was clear that the sin in my heart was Satan's work. So I was able to believe that God was working in me "to will and to do," while I was working out my own salvation "with fear and trembling" (Philippians 2:13, 12).

I became convinced that unbelief is voluntary and, furthermore, that it is a sin, since it makes God a liar (1 John 5:10). As the Holy Spirit convicted me of other sins in my life—especially that of preaching myself instead of Christ and indulging in self-congratulation after a sermon that pleased me—I was able to let go my pride and to seek only the honor that comes from God.

Satan put up a tremendous battle; but God finally showed me how to win the victory by living one day—one moment—at a time. I trusted in the blood of Jesus to atone for all my past sins, and I committed the future wholly to the Lord. I promised to do His will under all circumstances, as He made it known to me. Then I saw that all I had to do was to look to Jesus for my daily and hourly supply of grace, and to trust Him to keep me from sin *at the present moment.* Living in this moment-by-moment dependence upon the grace of Christ, I refused to permit Satan to trouble me about the past or the future.

I promised God, furthermore, that I would be a true son of Abraham and walk by faith in His Word—not by feelings and emotions. These still vary, but regardless of my feelings—or my lack of feelings—I praise God and trust in His Word.

Since that time the Lord has given me a steady victory over sins that had previously enslaved me. I delight in the Lord and in His Word. I delight in my work as a minister and in my fellowship with the Father and with His Son, Jesus Christ. Although I am still a babe in Christ, I think the Lord is beginning to revive His work among my people. Praise God!

May the Lord fill you with all His fullness (Ephesians 3:19) and give you the mind of Christ (1 Corinthians 2:16). The Lord loves you. He works with you. Rest your soul fully upon His promise, "Lo, I am with you alway, *even* unto the end of the world" (Matthew 28:20).

Your fellow soldier,

WILLIAM HILL

8
Difficulties Concerning Guidance

I am assuming that you have now begun the life of faith. You have given yourself totally to the Lord, and you are trusting Him to work His will in you. Your one desire is to do His will and to follow Him wherever He may lead you. But here you run into another difficulty. You haven't yet learned to know the voice of the Good Shepherd, and therefore you're not sure what *is* His will for you.

Perhaps God seems to be calling you into paths that your friends don't approve of. Some of these friends may have been Christians much longer than you and may seem to you to be much further advanced than you are. You respect their opinions and are hesitant to follow any guidance that doesn't concur with their ideas of what you should do. Yet you can't get rid of these impressions that have come to you—apparently from God—and you don't know which way to turn.

There is a solution to this problem, if you have really made a full surrender to God. I repeat *"full* surrender," because if you have held back anything, it will be almost impossible for you to hear what God is saying to you on that point.

The first thing, then, is to be sure that you really do desire above everything else to obey the Lord in all things. If this is the case, then you surely can't doubt His willingness to make His will known to you. The Bible contains clear promises on this point:

> . . . he calls his own sheep by name and leads them out. When he has brought out all his own, he goes before them, and the sheep follow him, for they know his voice.
>
> John 10:3, 4 RSV

Your Advocate, the Holy Spirit whom the Father will send in my name, will teach you everything, and will call to mind all that I have told you.

John 14:26 NEB

If . . . any of you does not know how to meet any particular problem he has only to ask God—who gives generously to all men without making them feel guilty—and he may be quite sure that the necessary wisdom will be given him.

James 1:5 PHILLIPS

These passages, and many more like them, make it clear that divine guidance is promised to us. Our part is to ask for it and then confidently expect it. James tells us that this confident faith is essential:

But let him ask in faith, with no doubting, for he who doubts is like a wave of the sea that is driven and tossed by the wind. For that person must not suppose that a double-minded man, unstable in all his ways, will receive anything from the Lord.

James 1:6–8 RSV

Accept the fact *right now* that divine guidance has been promised, and that you are sure to have it if you ask for it. Then don't allow yourself to be double-minded about your belief in God's willingness and ability to guide you.

Next, remember that our God has all knowledge and all wisdom. It is very possible, therefore, that the paths into which He guides you look very different in His eyes from the way they look to our shortsighted human eyes. God's thoughts are not man's thoughts, nor man's ways His ways (Isaiah 55:8). He alone can know from the beginning what the results of any course of action will be. Therefore His love for you may lead you in a direction that seems unwise to those who love you most here on earth.

Matthew 10:37–39; Luke 14:26–33; and other passages teach us that disciples of our Lord may be called upon to forsake inwardly all that they have, to turn their backs on those who are dearest to them, and in some cases to lay down their lives. (In these passages, Jesus is speaking of the requirements for *discipleship,* not for salvation. There is a distinction.) Unless the possibility of some disturbing guidance is clearly recognized, you may often have trouble hearing God's voice. Sooner or later the Christian who enters upon this life of obedience is likely to be led into paths which bring him into conflict with those he loves best. Unless he is prepared for this and can trust the Lord through it all, he will find it hard to follow the guidance he receives.

How *do* we receive guidance from God? How can we know His voice? There are four ways in which he reveals His will to us: (1) through the Scriptures, (2) through circumstances, (3) through our own best judgment, and (4) through inward impressions from the Holy Spirit. I call these four ways the four "voices" of God.

The Scriptures come first. If you are in doubt about any matter, consult the Bible about it (a concordance would be helpful) and see whether it contains any rule to guide you.

Until you have sought and obeyed God's will as revealed in His Word, you cannot expect a direct personal revelation.

Many serious mistakes are made in the matter of guidance when this simple rule is overlooked. Where God has written out for us a plain direction about something, He will not give us a special revelation in that matter. When we look for an inward voice instead of searching out and obeying the scriptural rule, we open ourselves to the deceptions of Satan and almost inevitably get into error.

For example, no man needs or could expect any direct revelation to tell him not to steal, because God has plainly declared His will about stealing in the Scriptures. I have met many Christians who have overlooked this rule of seeking God's guidance in His Word, and as a result have gone off into fanaticism.

I know, of course, that the Bible doesn't give a rule of action for every particular situation that arises, but there are not many *important* affairs in life which are not dealt with in God's Book. In many cases, the Scriptures are explicit even about details. For example, the Bible gives clear instructions concerning dress (1 Peter 3:3, 4; 1 Timothy 2:9); conversation (Ephesians 4:29; 5:4); revenge and self-protection (Romans 12:19–21; Matthew 5:38–48; 1 Peter 2:19–21); forgiveness (Ephesians 4:32; Mark 11:25, 26); conformity to the world (Romans 12:2; 1 John 2:15–17; James 4:4); and anxieties of all kinds (Matthew 6:25–34; Philippians 4:6, 7).

These examples are given to show what full and practical guidance the Bible provides. So whenever you are perplexed, first of all see whether the Bible speaks on the point in question. Ask God to let the Holy Spirit make plain to you what the Scriptures teach about His will in that matter. Then you must obey whatever seems to you to be the message of the Scriptures. God will never give special guidance about a point on which the Bible is explicit, nor could any "guidance" contrary to the Scriptures ever come from the Holy Spirit.

If a diligent search of the Bible doesn't give you any rule related to your difficulty, or if the directions given don't cover all the details of your case, then seek guidance from God's other "voices." Ask God for wisdom, as He tells us to do in James 1:5–7. If you ask in faith, He will answer your prayer by giving you a conviction based on your own best judgment, by arranging the circumstances of your life, or by giving you a clear inward impression. If the guidance is truly from God, all the answers received will harmonize, for God cannot say something in one voice and contradict it in another. Therefore, if you have an impression of duty, check it by (1) seeing if it is in accordance with Scripture, (2) asking whether your own higher judgment gives approval, and (3) waiting until, as we Quakers say, the "way opens" for you to carry it out.

If any of these checks is out of harmony, it is not safe to proceed. In this case, you must wait quietly, trusting the Lord to bring them all into harmony. You can depend on Him to do this sooner or later, if it is His voice that you are hearing. We must never forget that impressions can come from Satan as well as from the Holy Spirit. Therefore, anything which is out of harmony must be rejected.

Some earnest and honest Christians, with the mistaken idea that they were being led by the Holy Spirit, have ignored their own best judgment and have even violated the teachings of Scripture. God, seeing their sincerity, pities and forgives them; but He does not protect them from the sometimes disastrous consequences of their mistaken actions.

Every spiritual gift is linked with some element of risk, and this supreme blessing of direct guidance is no exception. Therefore we need to realize our own helplessness and to depend completely on the Lord to protect us against deception. The Christian who applies the checks I have mentioned and who commits the whole matter of guidance to the Lord with childlike trust has nothing to fear.

Now that I have pointed out the difficulties and risks involved, let me say something about the joy of having God's will communicated to us directly. It seems to me to be the grandest of all the privileges available to those whose life is "hid with Christ in God."

In the first place, it is wonderful just to know that God loves me enough to *care* about the details of my life. We never care about the little details of people's lives unless we love them. The daily activities of most people we meet are of no interest to us. But as soon as we begin to love someone, we begin at once to care about how that person spends his time. That God cares about my daily activities is proof of His love for me.

In the second place, it seems almost too good to be true that God is willing to let me know how to live and walk so as to please Him. What a privilege to have Him speak to me about my total life: my dress, my reading, my friendships, my occupations—everything that I do or think or say. If you would come into the full joy of this life of faith, you must experience this privilege for yourself.

God's promise that He will inspire "both the will and the deed, for his own chosen purpose" (Philippians 2:13 NEB) means that He will take possession of our will and make it work for us. His suggestions will come to us, not as commands from the outside but as desires arising from within. We shall feel that we *want* to do God's will—not that we *must* do it. Since it is always easy to do what we desire to do, our service to God becomes one of perfect freedom.

Every mother knows that her child would obey her perfectly if she could only get into that child's will and make him *want* to do the things she thinks he should do. This is what our Father does for His children who are walking with Him by faith: He writes His laws on our hearts and our minds (Hebrews 8:10; Jeremiah 31:33), so that we are drawn to obey them by our own inclinations and our judgment—not driven to obedience by fear.

The Holy Spirit's usual method of giving direct guidance is to impress upon the mind a wish or desire to do a certain thing, or to leave other things undone. Perhaps while you are praying, the thought may occur to you, "I would like to do thus-and-so; I wish I could." Turn this matter over to the Lord at once. Tell Him that it is your will to obey Him. Then, if the thing is in harmony with the Scriptures, with your own best judgment, and with circumstances, it is best to obey the leading immediately. It is always easiest to obey at the moment the Spirit speaks. If you hesitate and try to reason the thing out, obedience becomes harder and harder.

As a general rule, first impressions are the right ones in a fully surrendered heart, for God will make sure His voice is heard before any other voices. Therefore you should never try to reason about such impressions. It is safe to pray about them, but prayer must not be allowed to take the place of action.

If the suggestion doesn't seem clear enough to act upon, and especially if it doesn't agree with the advice of your Christian friends, then you may need to wait on the Lord for further light. But you must wait in faith, and in an attitude of entire surrender—continually saying *yes* to His will, whatever it may be. If the impression is from Him, it will grow stronger; if it is not from Him, it will disappear and you will forget you ever had it. If it comes to mind every time you try to pray and keeps you from having peace, you can be sure the impression is from God. If you don't obey it, your relationship with Him will suffer.

If the guidance is doubtful, the only safe thing to do is to yield the matter to God, until He clearly gives you the green light to take it back. Paul's rule about doubtful things is very explicit:

> I am convinced, and I say this as in the presence of the Lord Christ, that nothing is intrinsically unholy. But none the less it is unholy to the man who thinks it is . . . . Your personal convictions are a matter of faith between yourself and God, and you are happy if you have no qualms about what you allow yourself to eat. Yet if a man eats meat with an uneasy conscience about it, you may be sure he is wrong to do so. For his action

does not spring from his faith, and when we act apart from our faith we sin.

Romans 14:14, 22, 23 PHILLIPS

Surrender all doubtful things to God, until He gives you more light on His will concerning them. In most cases you will find that the doubt itself has been His voice calling you to conform more perfectly to His will.

Take all your questions to Jesus. Tell Him you only want to know and obey His voice, and ask Him to make it plain to you. Promise Him that you *will* obey, no matter what He may tell you to do. Believe implicitly that He is guiding you, as His Word promises He will. Listen for His voice continually, and the moment you are sure you hear it, *obey* it. Trust Him to make you forget the impression if it is not His will; then, if it continues and is in harmony with all His other voices, don't be afraid to obey.

Above everything else, *trust* Him! Faith is needed nowhere more than in this matter of guidance. God has promised to guide His children. You have asked Him to guide you. And now you must *believe* that He does and must take what comes as being His guidance. No earthly parent could guide his children if they refused to accept his commands as the real expression of his will. Likewise, God cannot guide *His* children if they never trust Him enough to believe that He is doing it.

I beg you not to be afraid to live each hour of every day under God's guidance. If He is trying to bring you out of the world and into a closer relationship to Himself, don't shrink from it. Such a relationship is a wonderful privilege. Rejoice in it! Embrace it eagerly. Let everything else go in order that it may be yours.

9

Difficulties Concerning Doubts

Many Christians are just as much enslaved by the habit of doubting as a drunkard is enslaved by alcohol. An army of doubts is constantly lying in wait for them and trying to block every inch of their spiritual progress. Doubt makes them miserable, hinders their usefulness, and continually breaks their fellowship with God.

In many cases entrance into the life that is "hid with Christ in God" sets the Christian free from his doubts. Sometimes, however, the old habit reasserts itself and brings setbacks and discouragement after weeks or months of steady progress in the life of faith.

If you have read *Pilgrim's Progress,* you may remember the story of Christian's imprisonment in Doubting Castle by the Giant Despair. When you read that story as a child and exulted in Christian's escape, you probably never suspected that you might find yourself taken prisoner by the same giant and imprisoned in the same castle. Yet I imagine that every Christian has been through at least one experience like this. If you can find a copy of *Pilgrim's Progress,* read it or reread it and see if you don't find that it describes experiences very much like some of your own.

It seems strange that people who call themselves believers should have to spend so much time in "Doubting Castle." Yet the habit of doubting is so universal that the term *doubters* is much more descriptive of most church members than the name *believers.* Unfortunately, most Christians have resigned themselves to their doubts as an affliction which is an inevitable part of this earthly life. They almost boast of their doubts as a man sometimes boasts of his rheumatism—trying to convince others that theirs is an "interesting case" with peculiar aspects deserving respect as well as sympathy.

Too often this description applies to believers who are sincere about wanting to enter the life of faith, and who have made some real progress in this direction. Some of them have gotten rid of their doubts about salvation and forgiveness for their sins, but they have not shaken the *habit* of doubting; they have simply shifted their doubts to a higher level. They say, "Yes, I believe my sins are forgiven and that I am a child of God through faith in Jesus Christ. I don't dare doubt this anymore. But then . . . ."

And this "but then" includes doubts about every promise God has made to His children. These chronic doubters refuse to believe any of them until they can have some more reliable proof than the simple word of God. And then they wonder why they have to walk in darkness! Many think of themselves almost as martyrs, and moan about the peculiar "spiritual conflict" they have to endure.

Spiritual conflict indeed! A much better name for it would be spiritual rebellion! Our fight is to be a fight of faith; the moment we doubt, our fight ceases and our rebellion begins.

I am sorry to say that I have no sympathy for such a chronic doubter. I would no more try to console him for his pitiful condition than I would weep with a drunkard and pray with him for grace to put up with his alcoholism. The only thing I would dare do for either one would be to tell him of the power of Jesus to set him free. Then I would beg and even command him to accept his freedom. I would say to him, "You ought to be free. You can be free. You *must* be free!"

Would you argue that it is inevitable for God's children to doubt Him? Is it inevitable for your children to doubt *you?* Would you put up with their doubts for a minute?

Would you sympathize with your son and feel that he was an "interesting case" if he came to you and said, "Dad, I can't believe your word. I can't trust your love"?

A friend of mine once left her two little girls with me while she did some shopping. The younger one, with childlike confidence, played happily until her mother's return. The older one, with the caution and mistrust of maturity, sat down in a corner to wonder whether her mother would remember to come back for her. Her fear that she would be forgotten led her to imagine that her mother would be glad of the chance to get rid of her anyhow, because she was such a bad girl. By the time her mother returned, she had worked herself into a frenzy of despair.

I'll never forget the look on my friend's face when her daughter, between sobs, told her what she had been imagining. Grief, wounded love, indignation, and pity all struggled for mastery.

The memory of that incident has come to my aid many times since then when doubts about my heavenly Father's love and care have tried to take control of my mind. Remembering the expression on that mother's face, I have rejected such thoughts before they could gain a foothold.

I am convinced that doubting is a real luxury to many people, and for such people to refrain from indulging in it would mean great self-denial. But indulgence in this luxury, as in some others, has unhappy consequences. When you think of the misery that doubting has caused you, you may deny vigorously that it is anything but a sore trial to you. But try giving it up, and you will soon find out whether it is a luxury.

Don't your doubts come knocking on your door like a group of sympathetic friends, who appreciate your hard case and have come to condole with you? And isn't it a luxury to sit down with them and entertain them, and listen to their arguments and accept their condolences? Wouldn't it be real self-denial to turn your back on them and refuse to hear a word they have to say? If you don't know, try it and see!

If you have ever indulged in the luxury of brooding on injustices other people have done you, you know how fascinating it is to think about their unkindness and to attribute all sorts of evil motives to their actions. This sort of thinking makes you miserable, of course; but it is so fascinating that you can't easily give it up. The luxury of doubting is just like this.

Things have gone wrong in your life. God has allowed you to have unusual temptations. Your case seems different from anyone else's, and you decide that God has forsaken you, that He doesn't love you, and doesn't care about your welfare. Soon you become convinced that you are too wicked for Him to care for, or too difficult for Him to manage. You don't blame Him or accuse Him of injustice, because you believe that you deserve His rejection and are unworthy of His love.

May I suggest that this false humility is nothing but a subterfuge which gives you freedom to indulge in the luxury of doubting. And may I suggest further that your thoughts about the Lord are just as displeasing to Him as if you *were* blaming Him for treating you unjustly. Jesus said He did "not come to call the righteous, but sinners" (Matthew 9:13); so your very sinfulness is your chief claim to His love and care.

What would you think of a sick man who said, "The doctor won't see me or give me any medicine, because I am sick. He only looks after healthy people"? Well, your line of reasoning is just as foolish! Jesus said, "It is not the healthy that need a doctor, but the sick" (Matthew 9:12 NEB). On another occasion He asked, ". . . If a man has a hundred sheep, and one of them has gone astray, does he not leave the ninety-nine on the hills and go in search of the one that went astray?" (Matthew 18:12 RSV). To think of Jesus as caring only for the persons who are spiritually healthy and for the lambs that never wander is far worse than to think unkindly of any earthly friend or foe.

From the beginning to the end of your Christian life, it is wrong to indulge in doubts. Doubts concerning God's promises are from the devil and are always untrue. The only way to meet them is by a direct and emphatic denial.

And now for the practical part of this chapter: how to get free from the habit of doubting. The answer is: in the same way you get release from any other sin—in Christ and *only* in Christ. You must do with your doubt just what you do with your other temptations—your temper or your pride, for example. You must hand it over to Jesus. Take a pledge against it, as a drunkard takes a pledge against alcohol, and trust in the Lord alone to make it possible for you to keep the pledge.

Like any other sin, doubt has its stronghold in the will. The *will to doubt* must be surrendered in just the same way as the will to yield to any other temptation. God always takes possession of a will surrendered to Him. If you say that you *will not doubt* and surrender to God your will in this matter, the Holy Spirit will immediately begin to work in you to keep you from doubting.

The trouble is that the doubter doesn't always make a full surrender, but often reserves a little secret liberty to doubt. You may even feel that it is actually a necessity at times.

"I don't want to doubt anymore," you say; or "I *hope* I won't." But it's hard to say, "I *will* not doubt again." No surrender can be effective until you reach the point of saying, "I will not." The option to doubt must be given up forever, and you must enter upon a life of continuous trust.

I think it is necessary to make a definite transaction of this surrender of doubting. It won't do to give it up by degrees. *Total abstinence* is the only method that will work for a drunkard or for a doubter.

Once this transaction has been made, you must depend completely upon the Lord for deliverance from each temptation to doubt. Lift up the shield of faith the moment the assault comes. When you feel the very first suggestion of doubt, hand it over to the Lord and tell Satan to settle the matter with Him. Don't listen to the doubt for a single moment, no matter how plausible it seems, or how well disguised as humility. Simply say, "I don't dare doubt; I must trust. The Lord is good, and He *does* love me. Jesus saves me. He saves me now."

Repeating over and over again those three little words, "Jesus saves me, Jesus saves me," will put to flight an army of doubts. I have tried it countless times, and it has never failed.

Don't argue with Satan or try to convince him that he is

wrong. Simply pay no attention to him. Shut the door in his face and emphatically deny every word he says to you. Bring up some "It is written" and throw it at him. Look steadily to Jesus and tell Him you trust Him and that you'll keep on trusting Him. No matter how strong the doubts may be, they can't hurt you if you won't let them in.

I know you'll sometimes feel that you are shutting the door against your best friends, and your heart will long to admit your doubts the way the Israelites longed for the fleshpots of Egypt. But deny yourself in this matter unrelentingly and refuse to let in a single doubt.

This very morning an army of doubts was lying in wait for me when I woke up, and they clamored at the door of my mind to be let in. Nothing seemed real or true; and what seemed most impossible of all was that I—weak, sinful *I*—could be the object of the Lord's love or care, or even of His notice.

It would have been a luxury to let these doubts in and invite them to take seats and make themselves at home in my mind. But years ago I made a pledge against doubting, and I would no more violate this pledge than I would violate my pledge against alcohol. Therefore I lifted up my shield of faith as soon as I became conscious of these suggestions, and handed the whole army over to my Lord to conquer. I began to say over and over, "God *is* my Father. I *am* His forgiven child, and He *does* love me. Jesus saves me; Jesus saves me now!"

The victory was complete. The enemy had "come in like a flood," but the Spirit of the Lord had lifted up "a standard against him" (Isaiah 59:19), and he was put to flight. Now my soul is singing the song of Moses and the children of Israel:

. . . "I will sing to the Lord, for he has triumphed gloriously; the horse and his rider he has thrown into the sea. The Lord is my strength and my song, and he has become my salvation; this is my God, and I will praise him, my father's God, and I will exalt him."

Exodus 15:1, 2 RSV

If you are having a battle against the habit of doubting, here is what I want you to do:

When you finish this chapter, take a pen and write down your resolution never to doubt again. Make it a real transaction between yourself and the Lord. Give up forever your freedom to doubt. Put your will in this matter on God's side, and trust Him to keep you from sinning in this way ever again. Tell Him how weak you are, how long you have encouraged the habit of doubt, and how helpless you are when it attacks you. Then commit the battle to Him. Tell Him you *will not* doubt again.

After you have done this, keep your eyes steadfastly on Jesus—away from yourself and away from your doubts. We are told to ". . . be firm and unswerving in the confession of our hope, for the Giver of the promise may be trusted" (Hebrews 10:23 NEB). "If only we keep our original confidence firm to the end," we "become Christ's partners" (*see* Hebrews 3:14 NEB) and will surely win the victory over doubt.

10

Difficulties Concerning Temptation

People who are trying to live the life of faith often misunderstand temptation.

The first mistake they make is to expect that no more temptations will come to them after they enter into the higher Christian life—that they have been freed not only from *giving in* to temptation but even from being tempted. Then when they find that temptations still come to them, they think they must have gone wrong in some way, and that their life isn't really "hid with Christ in God" after all.

A second mistake is to look upon temptation as sin and to blame themselves for what is entirely the work of Satan. This makes them feel condemned and discouraged; and if this state of mind continues, it leads eventually to actual sin. The discouraged person is an easy prey for Satan. Many Christians sin because they think they already *have* fallen!

The first of these mistakes could be avoided by recalling the Bible verses which state plainly that the whole Christian life is a warfare, for example, 2 Corinthians 10:3, 4; 1 Timothy 1:18; Ephesians 6:11–17. As a matter of fact, temptations usually grow *stronger* after we have entered into the higher Christian life. Strong temptations are generally a sign of great grace.

When the children of Israel first left Egypt, the Lord didn't lead them through the country of the Philistines (the nearest route); ". . . for God said, 'Lest the people repent when they see war, and return to Egypt'" (Exodus 13:17 RSV). Afterward, when they had learned more about trusting Him, He let their enemies attack them. But the battles they fought in the wilderness were insignificant in comparison with those they fought in the Promised Land. There they had to take walled cities, overcome giants, and conquer seven great nations and thirty-one kings. Likewise, the very power of your temptations may be proof that you really are in the Promised Land you have been seeking to enter. Therefore you must never let temptations make you question the fact that you *have* entered it.

The second mistake isn't quite so easy to deal with. Although it seems obvious that temptation is not sin unless we yield to it, many Christians are unable to grasp this fact. The very suggestion of wrong seems to bring pollution with it; and part of Satan's strategy is to make his intended victim feel that he must be very sinful to have such unholy thoughts even enter his mind.

Satan is like a burglar who breaks into a man's house to steal and, upon being caught, begins to accuse the owner himself of being the thief. Satan's favorite device is to come to us and whisper evil suggestions, doubts, blasphemies, and jealous, envious, or proud thoughts—and then say to us, "Oh, how wicked you are to think such things! Obviously you're not trusting the Lord, or these ideas would never have entered your mind." His reasoning sounds so plausible that the Christian often accepts it as true, and consequently feels condemned and discouraged. Then it is easy for Satan to lead him on into actual sin.

Nothing is more dangerous to the life of faith than discouragement, and nothing is more helpful than confidence. A very wise man once gave three rules for overcoming temptation:

1. Confidence
2. Confidence
3. Confidence

We must *expect* to conquer. That is why the Lord spoke so reassuringly to Joshua:

> Be strong and of a good courage.
> > Joshua 1:6, 9, 18
> Be not afraid, neither be thou dismayed.
> > Joshua 1:9
> Only be thou strong and very courageous.
> > Joshua 1:7

And this is why He says to us, "Let not your heart be troubled, neither let it be afraid" (John 14:27). Temptation would have no power over us if our courage remained high. Satan knows this well, and he always begins his attacks by discouraging us in any way he can.

Sometimes our discouragement arises from what we think is righteous grief and disgust with ourselves for allowing unholy things to tempt us. Actually, this disgust is not at all righteous, but comes from wounded self-love. We have been secretly congratulating ourselves that our tastes were too pure, our separation from the world too complete, for such temptations to come to us. When they do come, we are disappointed in ourselves and consequently discouraged.

Such discouragement is far more dangerous than the temptation which produced it. Although it masquerades as humility, it is not. The person with true humility can bear to see his own weakness and foolishness revealed, because he never expects anything from himself and knows that his only hope is in God. Instead of discouraging the Christian from trusting, true humility drives him to deeper trust. But the counterfeit humility produced by Satan leads to discouragement which is the very opposite of trust, and often drives its victim into the very sin that he despises.

I once heard an allegory that illustrates this point. Satan called a council of his servants to discuss what they could do to make a good man sin. One of his demons volunteered for the job, and Satan asked, "How will you do it?"

"I'll tempt him with the pleasures of sin. I'll tell him how much fun it is and what rewards it brings."

"That won't do," said Satan. "He has tried it and knows better."

Another evil spirit held up his hand and said, "I will make him sin."

"How?" asked Satan.

"I will tell him how foolish it is to be good and convince him that virtue brings no rewards."

"No, no!" exclaimed Satan. "That won't do at all. He has tried it and knows that wisdom's ways are 'ways of pleasantness, and all her paths are peace'" (Proverbs 3:17).

"Well," said another imp, "I will take on the job of making him sin."

"And what will *you* do?"

"I will discourage his soul," was the short reply.

"That will do it!" cried Satan. "*That* will do it! We'll conquer him now!"

And they did.

It is a true saying that "all discouragement is from the devil." I wish every Christian would memorize this maxim and never forget it. We must avoid discouragement as we would Satan himself.

But unless we recognize Satan's hand in the temptations that come to us, discouragement is inevitable. If we are to blame for our wicked thoughts, then we have every right to be discouraged. But we are *not* to blame. James says, "Blessed is the man that endureth temptation" (James 1:12), and "count it all joy when ye fall into divers temptations" (James 1:2). These verses remind us that temptation is not sin.

Actually, it is no more a sin to hear these whispers and suggestions of Satan than it is to hear blasphemy or obscenity from people whom we pass in the street. In either case sin comes only if we stop and join in. If we turn away from the wicked suggestions as soon as they come to us, as we would turn away from blasphemous talk, we are not sinning. But if we let our minds dwell on them and wonder if there might be some merit in them, then we are sinning.

We may be tempted by Satan a thousand times a day without sinning. But if he can succeed in making us think that *his* temptations are *our* sin, he has won half the battle and will very likely gain a complete victory.

A friend whom I will call Sadie once came to me in great distress about this very thing. She had been living the life of faith for some time, and had been so free from temptation that she had begun to think she would never be tempted anymore. But suddenly a very peculiar form of temptation began to torment her. The moment she began to pray, all kinds of dreadful thoughts would come into her mind.

Sadie had lived a very sheltered life, and these thoughts seemed so horrible to her that she felt she must be a terrible sinner to be capable of having them. In this way Satan first convinced her that she could not possibly have entered into the life of faith and finally deceived her into believing that she had never even been born again. She was in agony when she came to me.

I told her that these dreadful thoughts were nothing but the suggestions of Satan, that she was not to blame for them at all, and that she couldn't help them anymore than she could help hearing profanity spoken by people in her presence. I urged her to recognize them as coming from Satan and told her how to treat them. Instead of blaming herself or becoming discouraged, she was to turn at once to Jesus and commit them to Him. I showed her what an advantage Satan had gained by making her think that *she* originated these thoughts, and by filling her with self-condemnation and discouragement because of them. And I promised her complete victory if she would pay them no attention but would simply turn her back on them and look to the Lord.

Sadie was convinced, and the next time these thoughts came she said to Satan, "I recognize you this time! *You're* the one who has been suggesting these horrible thoughts to me. I hate them and will have nothing to do with them. The Lord is my helper; take them to Him and settle them in His presence!" Immediately Satan fled and the temptations ceased.

Another thing: Satan knows that a Christian is far more likely to reject a suggestion of evil if he knows it comes from the tempter than if it seems to come from his own mind. If Satan prefaced each temptation with the words, "I am Satan, your adversary; I have come to make you sin," few Christians would listen to his suggestions. To make his bait attractive, he has to hide himself. Therefore it is important that we become familiar with his tricks, so that we can recognize him the moment he comes to us.

There is still another mistake that many of us make about temptations—the mistake of thinking that all the time we spend in combating them is lost. For days at a time, we seem to make no progress in our Christian growth because we have to spend so much time fighting temptation. What we don't realize is that we may be serving God far more truly during these hours of temptation than in the times when Satan is leaving us alone.

Temptation is a manifestation of the devil's wrath against God more than against us. He can't touch our Savior, but he can wound Him by conquering us. Therefore we are really fighting our Lord's battles when we are fighting temptation, and under these circumstances hours may be worth days to us.

The verse that I quoted earlier—"Blessed is the man that endureth temptation"—surely means enduring continued and frequently recurring temptation. Nothing cultivates patience more effectively than the endurance of temptation; and nothing drives a Christian to complete dependence upon Jesus more surely than continued temptation. And finally, nothing brings more praise and honor and glory to our Lord Himself than our passing successfully the test of our faith which comes through temptations. Peter tells us that our faith is "infinitely more valuable than gold," which has to be "purified by fire" (*see* 1 Peter 1:7 PHILLIPS), and James promises that the man who patiently endures the temptations and trials that come to him will receive ". . . the crown of life which the Lord has promised to all who love him" (James 1:12 PHILLIPS). Small wonder, then, that Christians are urged to "count it all joy . . . when you meet various trials, for you know that the testing of your faith produces steadfastness. And let steadfastness have its full effect, that you may be perfect and complete, lacking in nothing" (James 1:2, 3 RSV).

It is plain that God uses temptation as a means of bringing us to perfection. This being so, Satan's own weapons are turned against himself—another example of the way *all* things (even temptations) "work together for good to them that love God" (Romans 8:28).

And now you may be asking, "But how do we overcome temptation?" If you have read this far, you should know that it is to be by faith, for faith is the foundation for all of the life that is "hid with Christ in God." Having started out to stand, walk, overcome, and live by faith, you have surely discovered your own utter helplessness and know by now that you can do nothing for yourself.

Therefore the only way to meet temptation is to hand it over to the Lord and trust Him to conquer it for you. But when you put it into His hands you must *leave* it there. Commit yourself to Him for victory over temptation as definitely as you committed yourself to Him for salvation. It was by faith alone then, and it must be by faith alone now. Thousands can testify that the Lord works miracles in conquering the temptations of those who trust Him completely.

But my purpose in this chapter isn't to show you how to gain victory over temptation, but simply to present temptation in its true light. I want to free conscientious, faithful Christians from the bondage into which they will surely be brought if, failing to understand the true nature of temptation, they confuse it with sin. Once they recognize Satan's hand in all their temptations, they should be able to say to him immediately, "Get thee behind me!" Then they can walk peacefully and triumphantly through his fiercest attacks, knowing that ". . . when the enemy shall come in like a flood, the Spirit of the Lord shall lift up a standard against him" (Isaiah 59:19).

11
Difficulties Concerning Failures

The title of this chapter may startle you. "Failures!" you say. "I thought there were no failures in this life of faith!"

My answer is that there ought not to be and need not be, but sometimes there are. And we have to deal with facts, not theories. It never becomes *impossible* to sin, even for Christians whose life is "hid with Christ in God." Although the possibility of a sinless life is available to them, there are very few who are not at times overcome by sudden temptation.

The sin I am talking about here is *conscious* sin. Sins of ignorance don't disturb our fellowship with God because they are all covered by the atonement. Please understand that everything I say in this chapter refers to sin which comes within the range of our consciousness. Understand, too, that I am not concerned with the doctrines concerning sin—these I leave to the theologians—but only with the believer's experience of sin.

Misunderstanding about conscious sin is dangerous to the believer who is trying to live the higher Christian life. When such a person realizes that he has sinned, he is likely to make one of two mistakes. He may become completely discouraged and give up the whole idea of living the life of faith; or he may feel it necessary to cover up his sin in order to preserve the theory on which this life is based.

Either of these courses is fatal to spiritual growth. The only way to handle the situation is to face the fact of sin, calling a spade a spade, and then try to discover the reason and the remedy. A life of union with God requires that we be absolutely honest with Him and with ourselves. Although the sin itself would cause only a momentary disturbance in our relationship with God, any dishonest dealing with it results in the loss of this fellowship.

115

A sudden failure is no reason for being discouraged and giving up on the life of faith. Neither does failure disprove what I have been teaching about this life. The higher Christian life is not a *state* but a *walk,* and the walk of faith is not a *place* but a *way.* Sanctification is not a possession that we acquire, once and for all, at a certain stage of our experience; it is a life to be lived day by day and hour by hour.

We may turn aside for a moment from a path we are following, but that doesn't obliterate the path and we can easily get back on it. Momentary failures in this walk of faith are most regrettable; but if we handle them in the right way, they should cause only a brief interruption in our communion with God and in our attitude of consecration and trust.

The important thing is an *immediate* return to God. Our sin is no reason to stop trusting, but only a sign that we need to trust more fully than ever. Whatever the reason for our failure, the remedy is certainly not discouragement. If a child falls when he is learning to walk, should he lie down and refuse to take another step? And should a believer who is trying to learn how to walk by faith give up in despair because he falls into sin? Of course not! In both cases the only thing to do is to get up and try again.

Soon after the children of Israel entered the Promised Land, they were disastrously defeated at the little city of Ai. Their reaction is described in the Book of Joshua:

> . . . At this the courage of the people melted and flowed away like water. Joshua and the elders of Israel rent their clothes and flung themselves face downwards to the ground; they lay before

the Ark of the Lord till evening and threw dust
on their heads. Joshua said, "Alas, O Lord God,
why didst thou bring this people across the Jordan only to hand us over to the Amorites to be
destroyed? If only we had been content to settle
on the other side of the Jordan! I beseech thee, O
Lord; what can I say, now that Israel has been
routed by the enemy? When the Canaanites and
all the natives of the country hear of this, they will
come swarming around us and wipe us off the
face of the earth. What wilt thou do then for the
honour of thy great name?"

Joshua 7:5–9 NEB

That wail of despair is echoed by many Christians whose
courage has "melted and flowed away like water" because
of a defeat by Satan. "If only we had been content to settle
on the other side of the Jordan!" is their feeling about
having entered into the life of faith. Like Joshua, they
predict further failures for themselves and complete victory for their enemies. They feel, as Joshua doubtless felt,
that discouragement and despair are the only proper reac-
tions to such a defeat.

But God thinks otherwise. "The Lord said to Joshua,
'Arise, why have you thus fallen upon your face?' " (Joshua
7:10 RSV). Joshua's position looked properly humble, but it
wasn't what God wanted. God told him to stand up, face
the evil, and get rid of it, and then "sanctify the people"
(*see* Joshua 7:13 RSV).

"Up, sanctify the people" is always God's command. "Lie
down and be discouraged" is always Satan's whisper. Our
feeling is that it is presumptuous—almost impertinent—to

go to the Lord right after we have sinned against Him. We feel that we ought to spend a little time flat on our faces, suffering for our sin. It seems unbelievable that the Lord *can* be willing to receive us back into His fellowship at once.

A little girl once expressed this feeling to me, with the candor typical of childhood. In reply to her question, "Does Jesus always forgive us for our sins as soon as we ask Him?" I had said, "Yes, of course He does."

"*Just* as soon?" There was doubt in her voice and on her face.

"Yes," I replied, "the very minute we ask, He forgives us."

She thought awhile and then said, "I can't believe that. I should think He would make us feel sorry for two or three days first. And then I should think He would make us ask Him lots of times, very politely. And I believe that *is* the way He does. You needn't try to make me think He forgives me at once, no matter *what* the Bible says."

This child put into words what most Christians think. What is worse, most Christians act on this belief. They let their discouragement and their remorse cause a much greater separation between them and God than their sin alone could have caused. They should know better—for what parent wants his children to act that way toward him? When a child has misbehaved, no loving mother wants him to go off alone in despair, doubting her willingness to forgive him. Her whole heart goes out to the child who runs to her and begs her forgiveness for the act of disobedience she has just discovered. Surely this is how God felt when He said to Israel, "Return, ye backsliding children, and I will heal your backslidings" (Jeremiah 3:22).

Ideally, the minute we are *conscious of having sinned, we*

ought to be conscious of being forgiven. In the walk of faith, no separation from God can be tolerated even momentarily, for the only way we can walk in this path is by looking continually to Jesus. The moment our eyes are taken off of Him to look at our own sin and weakness, we leave the path.

Therefore, if you have entered into this walk and find yourself overcome by sin, you must take it instantly to Jesus. Claim the promise in 1 John 1:9: "If we confess our sins, he is faithful and just to forgive us our sins, and to cleanse us from all unrighteousness." You must not hide your sin, try to excuse it, or push it out of your memory. Confess it to God, and believe then and there that God is faithful and just to forgive your sin and that He *does* do it. Believe also that He cleanses you from all unrighteousness. Claim immediate forgiveness and immediate cleansing, and then go on trusting more confidently than ever.

❧ ❧

Another thing: You must forget your sin as soon as it has been confessed and forgiven. Don't dwell on it, or you will soon magnify it into a mountain that hides Jesus from your eyes. Follow the example of Paul in ". . . forgetting what lies behind and straining forward to what lies ahead," and ". . . press on toward the goal for the prize of the upward call of God in Christ Jesus" (Philippians 3:13, 14 RSV).

Two contrasting cases illustrate the point I am trying to make.

The first is the story of George, an earnest Christian and an active church worker, who had been living the higher Christian life for several months when he suddenly realized that he was guilty of being unkind to a fellow

Christian. Since he had thought he could never sin again after having given his life completely to God, he was deeply discouraged. He decided that he must have been mistaken in believing he had entered into the life of faith. His discouragement increased until it led to a real depression, and he began to believe that he had never even been born again.

For three years George lived in misery, drawing further and further away from God and sinning in many different ways. His health failed, and he seemed to be in danger of losing his sanity.

Then one day he met Ruth, a Christian who had the same understanding of sin that I have been trying to convey. After talking with him for a while, she realized what his trouble was.

"You sinned in that act," she told him, "and I don't want you to try to excuse it. But haven't you confessed it to God and asked Him to forgive you?"

"*Confessed* it!" George exclaimed. "It seems to me I've done nothing for three years but confess it day and night, and beg God to forgive me."

"But you've never believed He did forgive you?"

"How could I?" asked George. "I've never *felt* forgiven."

"But suppose God *said* He forgave you. Would that convince you, even if you still didn't feel forgiven?"

"Of course," George replied. "If God said it, I'd have to believe it."

"Well, He *has* said it, right here in the Bible," was Ruth's answer. Turning to the first letter of John, she read the ninth verse aloud. "Now," she continued, "you say you have been confessing your sin for three years, and yet you have never believed God's promise that He is faithful and just to forgive you and to cleanse you. You have been making God a liar all this time."

The truth of what Ruth was saying suddenly dawned on George, increasing his sense of guilt. As he remained silent, Ruth suggested that they kneel down and that he confess his past unbelief and sin. When he had done this, she told him to claim, then and there, forgiveness and cleansing. He obeyed mechanically, but the result was glorious. In a few moments George was praising God aloud for setting him free from his burden of guilt. The three years of separation from God were wiped out in three minutes, and George once more began to enjoy the life that is "hid with Christ in God."

The other case is quite different. Diane had been living the life of faith for only two weeks when she gave way to a violent outburst of anger. For a moment discouragement threatened to overwhelm her. Satan said, "That shows it was all a mistake. You've been deceived about the whole thing. You haven't even entered into the life of faith, and you might as well stop trying. It's obvious that a life of holiness isn't for you!"

Fortunately, Diane had been given sound teaching on the higher Christian life. As soon as these thoughts entered her mind, she said, "Yes, I have sinned, and I am very sorry. But the Bible says that if we confess our sins, God forgives us and cleanses us—and I believe He will do it."

Even though she was still boiling with anger, she ran into her bedroom and knelt down beside the bed. There she confessed her sin to God and admitted that she was still angry. "I hate the anger, but I can't get rid of it," she told Him out loud. "I can only confess it to You and claim Your promise of forgiveness and cleansing."

The moment she finished praying, the Lord said, "Peace, be still," and Diane became calm. The calm was followed by a flood of light and joy, and she knew that she was both forgiven and cleansed of her anger.

The whole incident—the sin and the recovery from it—had taken less than five minutes, and Diane felt more secure than ever in her walk of faith.

In a spiritual crisis, the Christian's only hope is to trust the Lord. If this is all we *can do* and all we *ought* to do, isn't it better to do it at once? When I find myself seeking for some other way out of a crisis, I tell myself, "You'll have to come to simple trusting in the end. Why not try it *now*, in the beginning?" It is a life and walk of *faith* we have entered. If we stumble and fall on the path, the only way to recover is by an *increase* of faith, not a decrease.

Whenever you fall, then, remember to turn instantly to Jesus with a deeper consecration and trust. If you do that, your failures, regrettable as they are, will not break your fellowship with Him.

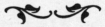

Now let's talk a little about the *causes* of failure in the higher Christian life. When you suffer a temporary defeat, don't put the blame on the strength of the temptation, on your own weakness, or, above all, on the Savior's inability or unwillingness to save you. The promise to Israel was positive: ". . . not a man shall be able to stand against you . . ." (Deuteronomy 7:24 RSV). And the promise to us is equally positive: ". . . God is faithful, and he will not let you be tempted beyond your strength, but with the temptation will also provide the way of escape, that you may be able to endure it" (1 Corinthians 10:13 RSV).

The men of Ai were "but few," and yet the army which had conquered the strong city of Jericho "fled before the men of Ai" (*see* Joshua 7:3, 4 RSV). It was not the strength of their enemy that defeated them; neither had God failed them. The Lord Himself told Joshua what caused their defeat:

> Israel has sinned: they have broken the covenant which I laid upon them, by taking forbidden things for themselves. They have stolen them, and concealed it by mingling them with their own possessions. That is why the Israelites cannot stand against their enemies . . . .
>
> Joshua 7:11, 12 NEB

It was a hidden evil that conquered Israel. Deep down under the earth, in an obscure tent in that vast army, were hidden some forbidden spoils of war. These few articles (stolen by one soldier) made the whole army helpless before their enemies. ". . . You have forbidden things among you, Israel; you cannot stand against your enemies until you have rid yourselves of them" (Joshua 7:13 NEB).

What does this Old Testament story have to teach about the cause of failure in the life of faith? Simply this: that anything in your heart which is contrary to the will of God, no matter how insignificant it may seem or how deeply it is hidden, will cause you to fall. Among the hidden things that may be responsible for paralyzing your spiritual life are resentment, self-seeking, harsh judgments of others, disobedience to the voice of the Lord, and any doubtful habits or associates.

The evil may be buried so deep in your subconscious mind that you fail to recognize its existence. Even though you are secretly aware of it all the time, you may ignore it and declare repeatedly that your life is *fully* consecrated to the Lord. If this is the case, no amount of church work, prayer, or understanding of the truth and beauty of the life of faith will prevent you from suffering repeated failures. The only thing that will do any good is to dig up the forbidden thing from its hiding place, bring it out into the light, and lay it before God. Therefore, the moment you meet with a defeat, you must look for the cause—not in the strength of that particular temptation, but in some hidden lack of consecration deep within your heart.

A headache is not a disease but only the symptom of a disease which may be centered in some other part of the body. Just so, conscious sin committed by a Christian may be only the symptom of an evil hidden in a very different part of his nature.

Sometimes the evil may be hidden in what appears on the surface to be a virtue. Apparent zeal for the truth may hide a spirit of criticism or intellectual pride. Apparent Christian faithfulness may hide an absence of Christian love. Apparent thrift and prudence in the management of our affairs may hide a lack of trust in God.

I believe the Holy Spirit is continually calling these things to our attention by little twinges and pangs of conscience, so that we really have no excuse for ignoring them. But it is easy to disregard these reminders and to insist that all is right within. As long as evil remains hidden in our hearts, it will cause defeat in the most unexpected places. An experience I had as a housewife serves as a parable to illustrate this truth.

I had moved into a new house and had given it, I thought, a thorough cleaning. In the basement I noticed a cider cask sealed at both ends. I considered having it taken out of the cellar so that I could open it to see what was in it. However, it seemed empty and looked clean. Furthermore, it was so large that I would need help to get it upstairs—so I decided to leave it alone. With every spring and fall housecleaning, the thought of that cask gave me a little twinge of housewifely conscience—which I managed to ignore.

For two or three years that innocent-looking cask stood quietly in my cellar. Then, for no apparent reason, I began having trouble with moths. I did everything I knew to get rid of them—even cleaned the carpet and had the furniture reupholstered—but the moths only multiplied faster.

Finally I thought of that cask in the basement. When I had it brought upstairs and opened it up, *millions* of moths poured out. At last I had found the cause of all my trouble.

Like that innocent-appearing cider cask, some apparently unimportant habit or indulgence may lie at the root of your failures in this higher Christian life. As long as you keep this forbidden thing hidden in the cellar of your subconscious mind, you will continue to suffer defeats at the hands of Satan. Although you have had little twinges of conscience about it now and then, you haven't yet brought it out into the light and investigated it under the searching eye of God.

Ask God to let His Holy Spirit bring to your mind any forbidden thing in your life that may be causing your spiritual problems. The prayer of David that concludes Psalm 139 is a good one for this purpose:

Search me, O God, and know my heart: try me, and know my thoughts: and see if there be any wicked way in me, and lead me in the way everlasting.

vv. 23, 24

Although I have written at length about failure, please don't think that I believe it is a necessary part of the Christian life. Jesus *is* able, as Zacharias prophesied, to deliver us "out of the hand of our enemies," that we "might serve him without fear, in holiness and righteousness before him, all the days of our life" (Luke 1:74, 75).

Never be satisfied until you are so pliable in God's hand and have learned to trust Him so completely that He will be able to "make you *perfect* in every good work to do his will, working in you that which is well-pleasing in his sight, through Jesus Christ; to whom be glory for ever and ever. Amen" (Hebrews 13:21).

12

Is God
in Everything?

Many people who are trying to live by faith find it almost impossible to believe that God controls everything. Most of them say they can submit to anything that comes from God, but not to the crosses that are put upon them by "man's inhumanity to man." They have trouble in trusting God, because situations that they have committed to Him often seem to be taken over and messed up by men.

Unless this difficulty can be overcome, the life of faith becomes an impossible and visionary theory. Nearly everything in life comes to us through other people, and most of our trials seem to be the result of somebody's failure, ignorance, carelessness, or sin. We know that God can't be the author of these things; but unless He has control over them, and over all things, how can we trust our lives and our loved ones to Him? How is it possible to live by faith if human agencies have the predominant influence in our lives? It would be foolish and even wrong to put our trust in them.

When we can see God's hand in a trial that comes to us, there is consolation and a certain sweetness in the thought that He cares enough about us to discipline us. But the trials inflicted by men contain nothing but bitterness.

Until we can see God in everything and receive everything as coming directly from His hands, we can never know complete consecration and perfect trust. We must consecrate ourselves to God, not to man, and our trust must be in Him, not in any "arm of flesh." Otherwise, we shall fail to meet the first trial that comes to us.

But *is* God in everything? Are we justified in receiving everything that comes to us as from His hands, regardless of the second causes that may be involved?

To these questions I answer unhesitatingly, *yes*. Everything that comes to the children of God comes directly from their Father's hand, no matter who or what may have been the apparent agent. There are no "second causes" for us. This is the whole teaching of the Scripture.

Because this belief is so hard for many Christians to accept, I am listing below a few of the many passages of Scripture that support it. Store them in your memory now, and they will be like a bank account on which you can draw when trouble comes.

"Are not sparrows two a penny? Yet without your Father's leave not one of them can fall to the ground. As for you, even the hairs of your head have all been counted."

Matthew 10:29, 30 NEB

Cast all your cares on him, for you are his charge.

1 Peter 5:7 NEB

The Lord is on my side; I will not fear: what can man do unto me?

Psalms 118:6

. . . If God is on our side, who can ever be against us?

Romans 8:31 LB

The Lord is my shepherd; I shall not want.

Psalms 23:1

When you pass through the waters I will be with you; and through the rivers, they shall not overwhelm you; when you walk through fire you shall not be burned . . . .

Isaiah 43:2 RSV

He changes times and seasons; he removes kings and sets up kings . . . .

Daniel 2:21 RSV

The king's heart is a stream of water in the hand of the Lord; he turns it wherever he will.

Proverbs 21:1 RSV

The Lord brings the plans of nations to nothing; he frustrates the counsel of the peoples. But the Lord's own plans shall stand for ever, and his counsel endure for all generations.

Psalms 33:10, 11 NEB

Whatever the Lord pleases he does, in heaven and on earth, in the seas and all deeps.

Psalms 135:6 RSV

Have you not known? Have you not heard? The Lord is the everlasting God, the Creator of the ends of the earth. He does not faint or grow weary, his understanding is unsearchable.

Isaiah 40:28 RSV

God is our refuge and strength, a very present help in trouble. Therefore will not we fear, though the earth be removed, and though the mountains be carried into the midst of the sea; Though the waters thereof roar and be troubled, though the mountains shake with the swelling thereof.

Psalms 46:1–3

He who dwells in the shelter of the Most High, who abides in the shadow of the Almighty, will say to the Lord, "My refuge and my fortress; my God, in whom I trust." For he will deliver you from the snare of the fowler and from the deadly pestilence; he will cover you with his pinions, and under his wings you will find refuge; his faithfulness is a shield and buckler. You will not fear the terror of the night, nor the arrow that flies by day, nor the pestilence that stalks in darkness, nor the destruction that wastes at noonday. A thousand may fall at your side, ten thousand at your right hand; but it will not come near you . . . . Because you have made the Lord your refuge, the Most High your habitation, no evil shall befall you, no scourge come near your tent. For he will give his angels charge of you to guard you in all your ways.

Psalms 91:1–7, 9–11 RSV

. . . Be satisifed with what you have. For God has said, "I will never, *never* fail you nor forsake you." That is why we can say without any doubt or fear, "The Lord is my Helper and I am not afraid of anything that mere man can do to me."

Hebrews 13:5, 6 LB

These Scriptures and many others like them make it clear that second causes and human agencies have no power over the children of God. All these things are under the control of our Father, and none of them can touch us except with His knowledge and by His permission. Nothing that originates in the sin of man can be said to be the will of God—but *by the time it reaches us, it has become God's will for us,* and we must accept it as coming directly from His hands. No man or company of men, no power in earth or heaven can touch any person who is abiding in Christ, without first passing through Him and receiving His permission. If God is for us, it doesn't matter who is against us: nothing can disturb or harm us unless He sees that it is best for us and stands aside to let it pass.

An earthly parent's care for his child gives only a feeble illustration of God's care for us. Without your consent, nothing can touch your baby when he is in your arms, unless you are too weak to ward it off. And if you *are* too weak, you will sacrifice your life, if necessary, in an effort to keep your child from being hurt. If an earthly parent would go to such extremes to protect his child from harm, how much more will our heavenly Father protect us, His children! His love is infinitely greater than that of any mortal father, and His strenth and wisdom are unlimited.

Some of God's own children seem to think that they are more tender, loving, and caring than He is. They secretly accuse Him of neglecting them and being indifferent to their welfare. The truth is that His care is infinitely superior to any possible human care. If He counts the hairs on our heads and doesn't allow even a sparrow to die without His permission, we can know that He observes and controls even the smallest circumstance that affects the lives of His children, no matter where that circumstance originates.

The Bible contains many examples of God's providential

care for His children. Joseph's life is one. When his brothers sold him into slavery, he must have felt that God had His back turned and was allowing evil to have its way with him. Years later, however, he learned what God's purpose had been and told his brothers, ". . . You meant evil against me; but God meant it for good . . ." (Genesis 50:20 RSV). "Do not be distressed, or angry with yourselves, because you sold me here; for God sent me before you to preserve life" (Genesis 45:5 RSV).

The action of Joseph's brothers was unquestionably evil; but by the time it reached Joseph, it had become God's will for him. The ultimate result was blessing, not only for Joseph, but even for his sinful brothers. This story shows that God can make even the wrath of man praise Him (Psalms 76:10) and that *all* things, even the sins of others, "work together for good to them that love God" (Romans 8:28).

Long before I knew the Scriptures that teach this truth, I became a firm believer in it through a testimony given at a prayer meeting I was attending. The speaker told how hard it had been for her to live the life of faith because of the "second causes" that seemed to control the circumstances surrounding her. This problem became so perplexing to her that she began to ask God to show her whether or not He really is in everything.

After she had been praying in this way for a few days, she had a vision. In it she saw herself in a dark place, with a body of light some distance away. This light came toward her and gradually surrounded her. As it approached, she heard a voice saying, "This is the presence of God. This is the presence of God."

While she was surrounded with this light, all the

frightening things she could imagine seemed to pass before her: fighting armies, wicked men, raging beasts, fearful storms, and pestilences—sin and suffering of every kind. At first she shrank back in terror; but she soon saw that each one of these things was enveloped by the presence of God. No lion could attack, no bullet fly through the air, unless the presence of God moved out of the way to permit it. As long as the thinnest sheet of this glorious presence stood between her and the threatening things, none of them could touch her.

Next, all the small and annoying things of life passed before her. These too were enveloped in this presence of God. Not a cross look, a harsh word, or a petty annoyance of any kind could reach her unless God's presence moved out of the way to let it pass through.

This vision answered her question forever. Now she knew that God *is* in everything—and to her there were no longer any second causes. She saw that her life came to her day by day and hour by hour directly from the hand of God, no matter what "middlemen" seemed to control it. Never again did she have any difficulty in yielding totally to His will and trusting completely in His care.

How I wish it were possible to make every Christian see this truth as plainly as I see it! I am convinced it is the key to a completely restful life. Nothing else will enable a person to live in the present moment, as we are commanded to do, and to "take . . . no thought for the morrow" (Matthew 6:34). Nothing else will take all the risks and "supposes" out of a Christian's life and enable him to say with certainty, "Surely goodness and mercy shall follow me all the days of my life" (Psalms 23:6). Under God's care we run no risks.

Nancy is a joyous, triumphant Christian who earns a precarious living by doing day work. One of her employers is a gloomy Christian who disapproves of Nancy's constant cheerfulness almost as much as she envies it. One day she said to her, "Nancy, I don't see how you can be so happy when you think about your future. Suppose you should get sick and be unable to work, or suppose some of the people you work for should move away, and no one else would give you a job. Or suppose . . . ."

"Stop!" Nancy said. "I never 'suppose.' The Lord is my Shepherd, and I know I shall not want. And, honey," she added, "it's all those 'supposes' that are making you so miserable. You'd better give them all up and just trust the Lord."

Nothing else but seeing God in everything can make us loving and patient with those who annoy us. When we realize that they are only the instruments for accomplishing His purpose in our lives, we will actually be able to thank them (inwardly) for the blessings they bring us.

Nothing else will put an end to all grumbling and rebellious thoughts. Christians who would never dare to grumble about God often don't hesitate to grumble about the circumstances of their lives and to rebel against those whom they hold responsible for those circumstances. But this way of receiving all things as coming from God makes it impossible ever to grumble or rebel. If our Father permits a trial to come to you, it must be because it is the best thing that could happen to you. Therefore you must accept it with thanks as coming from His hand. I'm not saying that you must like or enjoy the trial; but you must accept it with gratitude because God is using it to work out

His purpose for your life—and His purpose is always for your ultimate good.

Seeing our Father in everything makes life one long thanksgiving. If God's will is your will and if He always has His way, then you always have your way also. If you side with God, you cannot fail to be victorious in every encounter. Whether the result is joy or sorrow, failure or success, death or life, you will be able to say, with Paul, "But thanks be to God, who in Christ always leads us in triumph . . ." (2 Corinthians 2:14 RSV).

13

Bondage or Freedom?

There are two kinds of Christian experience: one of bondage and one of freedom.

In the first, the believer obeys the law of God from a sense of duty, from fear of punishment, or from expectation of reward. In the second, the controlling power is within him and causes him instinctively to follow the divine Life-giver. The first type of Christian is a servant, who works for hire; the second is a son, who works for love.

To live in freedom is the privilege and right of every Christian. Why, then, do so many of God's children live in bondage? The answer to this question is *legalism,* and the remedy for legalism is Jesus.

In the Epistle to the Galatians these two forms of Christian experience are fully described and contrasted. Paul wrote this letter when he learned that some Judaizers (Jewish Christians who thought Gentile converts should conform to the religious practices of the Jews) had come among the churches in Galatia, teaching that certain rites and ceremonies were necessary to salvation. In this way they had succeeded in drawing the Galatians away from the freeing power of the Gospel.

The Galatians' sin was spiritual rather than moral. They had developed a wrong attitude toward God—a legalistic attitude. Like most Christians, they had begun right, having entered into the spiritual life by hearing and believing the Gospel (*see* Galatians 3:2 TEV). But when it came to living this life, they had changed their ground and had sought to substitute works for faith. Having begun by God's Spirit, they were now trying to finish by their own power (*see* Galatians 3:3 TEV).

Let me try to illustrate how these two attitudes differ. Here are two men, neither of whom steals. In their actions,

141

they are equally honest; but in their motives they are vastly different. One man has a dishonest nature and is deterred from stealing only by the fear of punishment; the other is so honest that he could not be induced to steal, even by the promise of a reward. The second is honest within; the first is honest only in his outward behavior.

The application of this parable to Christian life is obvious; yet we are continually tempted to forget that the vital matter is not what men *do* but what they *are*. God is not concerned with our legal observances but with our being "new creatures" (Galatians 6:15; 2 Corinthians 5:17). He knows that if we *are* right we shall certainly *do* right. It is possible to do right without being right at all; but this kind of doing has no vitality in it and is of no real value.

Paul was grieved with the Galatian Christians because they seemed to have lost sight of this vital truth. They had begun as new creatures, but had "fallen from grace" (Galatians 5:4) and were trying to serve God under the "old written code" rather than in the "new life of the Spirit" (*see* Romans 7:6 RSV). Paul gave them fair warning: "Those of you who try to be put right with God by obeying the Law have cut yourselves off from Christ. You are outside God's grace" (Galatians 5:4 TEV).

The Galatians had made the mistake of thinking that something else besides Christ was necessary for them to live as Christians. The Judaizers who had come among them had taught them that Jesus alone was not enough for salvation, but that obedience to the ceremonial law must be added. They had therefore imported some ceremonies out of the Jewish ritual and had tried to compel the Gentiles to live like Jews.

Modern Christians are greatly surprised at the Galatians and wonder how they could have fallen prey to such legalism. But doesn't the same temptation, under a different form, exist today? The Galatians added the ceremonial law; *we* add dress codes, creeds, Christian work, churchgoing, or religious rites of one sort or another. It doesn't make much difference what you add; the mistake is to add anything at all to a saving faith in Jesus.

We condemn the Judaizers' religion because, by depending upon outward deeds and ceremonies to bring salvation, it rejects the grace of God and ". . . means that Christ died for nothing!" (Galatians 2:21 TEV). But I fear that we reject the grace of God by our legalism just as surely as they did by theirs.

The following contrast may help to clarify the distinction between a religion of bondage and a religion of freedom. Perhaps it will also show you where you yourself may be bound by legalism. (The italics are added to the Scripture quotations.)

The Law Says	The Gospel Says
Do this, and you will live (Leviticus 18:5).	*Live,* and then you will do.
Pay what you owe (Matthew 18:28).	He frankly *forgives* you all (Luke 7:42).
"*Make* you a new heart and a new spirit" (Ezekiel 18:31).	"I will *give* them a different heart and put a new spirit into them . . ." (Ezekiel 11:19 NEB).
"*Love the Lord* your God with all your heart, with all your soul, and with all your strength" (Deuteronomy 6:5 TEV).	"This is what love is: it is not that we have loved God, but that *he loved us* and sent his Son to be the means by which our sins are forgiven" (1 John 4:10 TEV).

"God's *curse* [is] on anyone who does not obey all of God's laws and teachings" (Deuteronomy 27:26 TEV).

"The *wages* of sin is death" (Romans 6:23).

"*Blessed* are they whose iniquities are forgiven, and whose sins are covered" (Romans 4:7).

"The *gift* of God is eternal life through Jesus Christ our Lord" (Romans 6:23).

Do.
If . . . .

Done.
Therefore . . . .

The Law

Demands holiness.
Extorts the unwilling service of a slave.
Makes blessings the result of *obedience.*
Places the day of rest at the *end* of the week's work.
Was given to *restrain* the old nature.

The Gospel

Gives holiness.
Wins the loving service of a son.
Makes obedience the result of *blessings.*
Places it at the *beginning.*

Was given to bring *freedom* to the new nature.

Under the Law

Salvation was *wages.*

Under the Gospel

Salvation is a *gift.*

Paul tells us that the law is not our savior but our schoolmaster, for the purpose of bringing us to Christ. After we have put our faith in Jesus, he declares, "we are no longer under a schoolmaster" (Galatians 3:25).

To illustrate his meaning, Paul uses the contrast between a servant and a son. Now that we are no longer servants but sons (Galatians 4:7), he entreats us to stand fast in the freedom Christ has given us, and not to be "entangled again with the yoke of bondage" (Galatians 5:1).

A woman who is a servant in a house is paid for her work in weekly wages, and works according to the rules laid down by her employer. She might try to please him, but only out of a sense of duty. Suppose, however, that her employer falls in love with her and changes her status from that of a maid to that of his wife.

At once the whole spirit of her service is changed. She may continue to do the same things she did before, but she does them now from an entirely different motive. The old sense of duty is replaced by love. The cold word *employer* is transformed into the loving word *husband*. "And it shall be at that day, saith the Lord, that thou shalt call me Ishi [my husband]; and shalt call me no more Baali [my lord]" (Hosea 2:16).

Now suppose that this wife, thinking back upon her past position, is so overwhelmed by an inferiority complex that she loses the inward sense of union with her husband. Very soon the joy of working because of love for her husband would be gone, and in spirit she would be working again for the wages of an employer.

Such a woman would be foolish indeed. But aren't many Christians just as foolish? Thinking of God as a stern taskmaster who demands their obedience—not as the loving Father who wins it—they serve Him, not out of love, but from a sense of duty and fear.

This legalistic spirit destroys the sweetness of any relationship. When a husband and wife cease to perform their services to each other in love and begin to carry them out from a sense of duty alone, the marriage tie becomes enslaving, and acts that were once a joy become "crosses."

Many Christians think that taking up the cross means doing something they ought to do but dislike doing—and they may even feel that such distasteful service is particularly pleasing to God. But would any man be pleased if his wife said to him every morning as he left for work, "I am going to clean the house and cook dinner for you today, but I want you to know that I despise doing these chores"? No wonder Paul was alarmed when he found that this legalistic spirit was creeping into the churches in Galatia.

Legalistic Christians do not actually deny Jesus; they only seek to add something to Him. Their idea is "Jesus *and* . . . ." Perhaps it is Jesus and good works, Jesus and deep emotion, Jesus and correct doctrine, or Jesus and certain religious rites. These things may be good in themselves, and *are* good when they are the fruits of salvation, but to add *anything* to Christ as a *requirement* for salvation is to deny His completeness and exalt oneself.

Rather than admit helplessness, men will undergo many painful sacrifices, if only self may share the glory. A religion of bondage always exalts self. It is what *I* do—*my* efforts, *my* fasting, *my* sacrifices, *my* prayers. But a religion of freedom leaves nothing for self to glory in: it is all Christ, and what He does, and what He is, and how wonderfully He saves. Our boast is in the Lord (Psalms 34:2) when, in this life of freedom, we come to know that He and He alone is the sufficient supply for our every need.

Since we are the children of God and also His heirs (Romans 8:17), there is no need for us to work for our inheritance from our Father. But how few Christians act like the heirs of God! Most of us seem to be poverty stricken, and work hard for the little we do possess.

You may feel that good has come from your self-effort

or your asceticism. Such behavior does indeed have ". . . an air of wisdom, with its forced piety, its self-mortification, and its severity to the body . . ." (Colossians 2:23 NEB), but I am convinced that any *real* good that has come to you has come in spite of your legalistic behavior and not because of it.

Bessie is a friend of mine whose Christian life was one of bondage. She asked me one day what I thought Jesus meant when He said that His yoke is easy and His burden light (Matthew 11:30); she had certainly not found it so! She worked harder for her salvation than any slave ever worked to purchase his freedom. No day, she felt, could go right for her or for any member of her family unless she began it by spending long hours on her knees in agonized prayer.

I told her that I thought she must have gotten things wrong somehow, for I didn't find in my Bible any suggestion that wrestling and agonizing were necessary for a right relationship with God.

"What would you think," I asked her, "of parents who made their children plead with them every morning for their food and clothing, or of a shepherd whose sheep had to battle with him in order to secure proper care?"

"That would be all wrong, of course," she replied, "but why do I have such *good* times after I have gone through these conflicts?"

This question puzzled me until I asked, "What finally happens to bring about those good times?"

"Why, I finally come to the point of trusting the Lord," was her reply.

"Suppose you came to that point to begin with?"

Bessie's face was suddenly illuminated. "I never until

this minute thought I might!" she exclaimed joyfully.

Unless we become like children, Jesus said, we cannot enter the Kingdom of Heaven (Matthew 18:3). But it is impossible to have the spirit of a child until the spirit of slavery has disappeared. Notice that I said the spirit of *slavery,* not the spirit of *service.* Every good child is filled with the spirit of service, but no child should have a spirit of slavery. The child serves from love; the slave works from fear and necessity.

If your son should get the idea that you would not give him food and clothing unless he earned them in some way, the relationship between you would be destroyed. Legalistic Christians grieve the heart of their heavenly Father when they let the spirit of slavery creep into their relationship with Him. As soon as we begin to "work for our living" in spiritual things, we have stepped out of the son's place into that of the slave. In so doing, we have fallen from grace.

In His parable of the talents (Matthew 25:14–30), Jesus condemned the servant who thought his lord was a hard master; yet Christians who are under a spirit of bondage feel the same way about God. Too many believers have bowed their necks to the yoke of Christ as if it were a yoke of slavery. To them, His declaration that His yoke is easy sounds like a fairy tale, and they never dream that it was meant to be realized as a fact.

The concept of the Christian life as a life of bondage is deeply ingrained in the church—so much so that the child of God who finds himself living in freedom often begins to think there must be something wrong in his experience. No longer can he find a cross to bear! The Christian who feels this way is just as much in error as the wife who thinks she doesn't love her husband when she finds that she enjoys all the services she performs for him.

Sometimes I think the whole secret of the Christian life that I have been trying to describe is to be found in the child's relationship with his parents. To live a joyful life, the follower of Jesus need only believe that God is as good a Father as the best father on earth, and that a Christian's relationship to God is just the same as that of a child to his earthly parents.

Children do not need to carry around in their own pockets the money for their support. If they did, they would probably lose it. In the same way, it isn't necessary for the Christian to try to maintain all his spiritual possessions in his own keeping. God has wisely provided for our riches to be stored up for us in Christ. Then, when we want anything, we can receive it direct from His hands. ". . . God has made him our wisdom; he is our righteousness; in him we are consecrated and set free" (1 Corinthians 1:30 NEB). Apart from Him we have nothing.

To receive a valuable gift from a comparative stranger often makes one uncomfortable. But when two people are united in love, gifts of great value may be exchanged with no feeling of embarrassment or obligation on either side.

This principle holds true in the spiritual life as well. When Christians are living far from God, they find it hard to accept any great blessing from Him, even when He puts it in their laps. They feel so unworthy that they aren't even able to recognize it as being theirs, and they go on their way without it. But when Christians get close enough to the Lord to feel the true spirit of adoption, they realize how eager He is—as good parents always are—to pour out good gifts upon His children. Accepting with delight all the blessings He has for them, they discover that all things are theirs, because they are Christ's and Christ is God's (1 Corinthians 3:22, 23).

The life "hid with Christ" is no great mystery, as some people want to make it. It is simply a matter of choosing freedom instead of bondage. It is only finding out that we really are no longer slaves but sons (*see* Galatians 4:7 RSV), and then enjoying all the privileges of sonship.

God did not use the figure of father and children without knowing all that this relationship implies. Therefore, those who know Him as their Father know the whole secret. They are their Father's heirs and may enter *immediately* into possession of everything they need for the present moment.

Legalistic Christians are in bondage because they do not understand that their relationship to God is that of children to a father, and do not recognize that He loves them even more than any earthly father can. If they did recognize this truth and accept it, the spirit of bondage could not exist. Our freedom, therefore, is dependent upon our understanding the mind and thoughts of God toward us.

What are the facts in the case? If God has called us only to be slaves, then the Christian life is indeed one of weary bondage. But if He has called us to be children and heirs, how it must grieve Him to see us submitting to a yoke of slavery, no matter how worthwhile a yoke it may seem to be!

The idea of slavery is utterly incompatible with any relationship that is based on love, whether that relationship is earthly or heavenly. While the poor enslaved Christian will finally enter into his heavenly rest, I fear that he will be in the sad condition of those described in 1 Corinthians 3:11–15. They will be saved, but their work will be burned and they themselves will suffer loss.

"Against such there is no law" is the divine sentence concerning the fruit which the Spirit produces in a human life (Galatians 5:23). If you will give up all self-effort and self-dependence and will just let Jesus live in you, work in you, and be your indwelling life, spiritual fruit will soon take the place of legalistic work.

The man who is controlled and empowered by the Holy Spirit is not under bondage to outward requirements; but the one who attempts to live by a set of rules and lacks the inward restraint of the Spirit of Christ is a slave to the law. The first man is free because he fulfills the law in his inmost being. The other rebels inwardly against the law and is therefore bound by it.

14
Growth

Some people seem to think that teachings about the life of faith are incompatible with the doctrine of "growth in grace." They believe that advocates of this life are saying that the believer arrives immediately at a state of perfection and has no further to go. If this were the case, the Scriptures that stress continued growth and development would have no meaning. In this chapter I hope to be able to answer such objections fully, and also to show what the Bible teaches about where and how the soul is to grow.

The text most frequently quoted relative to growth is 2 Peter 3:18: "Grow in grace, and in the knowledge of our Lord and Saviour Jesus Christ." This text expresses what I believe to be God's will for us, and what He enables us to experience. I accept, in their very fullest meaning, all the commands and promises related to our growing up into Christ, until we come ". . . to mature manhood, measured by nothing less than the full stature of Christ" (Ephesians 4:13 NEB). How wonderful that we need not continue always to be "infants in Christ," needing milk (*see* 1 Corinthians 3:1, 2 NEB); but that we may, by reason of growth, become mature Christians who "can take solid food" (*see* Hebrews 5:14 NEB). It would grieve me to think that a Christian's growth in this life had an end point beyond which he could advance no further.

The kind of growing I believe in is the kind that actually leads to maturity; and the development I believe in is that which eventually brings forth ripe fruit. Jesus sets this goal before us, and I expect to reach it. There is something wrong with growth that doesn't lead to maturity and to fruit bearing. No parent would be satisfied with the growth of a child who remained a helpless infant day after day and year after year. And no farmer would be content with

155

corn that never produced an ear.

Growth, to be real, must lead to progressive development and increasing maturity. Too often, however, the very Christian who most longs for spiritual growth and makes the greatest efforts to attain it finds at the end of a year that he has gone backward rather than forward. His zeal, his devotion, and his separation from the world are likely to seem less whole-souled and complete than when he first became a Christian.

Once I was talking to a group of Christians about the privileges and rest to be gained by an immediate and definite step into the life of faith. A very intelligent woman interrupted me by exclaiming, "But, Mrs. Smith! I believe in *growing* in grace!"

"How long have you been growing?" I asked.

"About twenty-five years," was her reply.

"And are you more unworldly and more devoted to the Lord now than you were when you first began?" I pressed her.

Her face fell. "Not nearly so much so, I'm afraid."

This answer opened her eyes to the truth that, even though she *believed* in growing in grace, she had not been *doing* it.

The trouble with this woman, as with many other Christians, is that she was trying to grow *into* grace, rather than *in* it. She was like a rosebush planted in a hard, stony path, trying to grow into the flower bed. It naturally withers and dies instead of flourishing and maturing. *If we are to grow in grace, we must first be planted in grace.*

Another picture of this ineffective sort of "growing" is given by the children of Israel during their years of wandering in the wilderness. After forty years of traveling, they were no nearer the Promised Land than they were at the beginning. Kadesh-barnea, where they started, was at the border of the land, and a few steps would have taken them into it. When they ended their wanderings in the plains of Moab, they were again at its borders; but this time they had a river to cross. All their wanderings and battles in the wilderness had not given them possession of one inch of the Promised Land. Before they could begin to possess it, they had to step into it. Once they were in the land, their conquest of it was very rapid.

In the same way the soul, once it is planted in grace, grows more in one month than it could grow during years in any other soil. For grace is a most fruitful soil, and the plants that grow in it are tended by a divine Gardener, warmed by the sun of His presence, and watered by the dew and rain from His heaven. It is no wonder that they bring forth fruit, "some an hundredfold, some sixtyfold, some thirtyfold" (Matthew 13:8).

What do I mean by "growing in grace"? This question is a hard one to answer, because so few people have any concept of what the grace of God really is. To say that it is free, unmerited favor expresses only a little of its meaning. It is the wonderful, boundless love of God poured out upon us without stint or measure. It is given, not according to our deserving, but according to His infinite love, the love which Paul describes as being "beyond knowledge," so immeasurable are its heights and depths (*see* Ephesians 3:18, 19 NEB).

Some people seem to think of God's love as being totally different from human love—somehow less personal and less real. But if ever human love was tender, self-sacrificing, and devoted, divine love is infinitely more so, and infinitely more forgiving, more willing to suffer for its loved ones, and more eager to lavish the best gifts and blessings upon them. Put together all the tenderest love you know of—the deepest you have ever felt and the greatest that has ever been given you; heap upon it all the love of all the loving human hearts in the world; multiply it by infinity. Only then will you *begin* to have some faint idea of the love of God in Christ Jesus. And *this is grace*.

To be planted in grace is to live in the very heart of this love—to be enveloped by it and steeped in it; to know nothing but this love now and forever; to learn more about it and have greater faith *in* it day by day; to entrust everything to its care; and to know without the shadow of a doubt that it will order all things well.

To grow in grace is opposed to all self-dependence, all legalism of every kind. It is to put our growing, along with everything else, into the hands of the Lord, and to leave it with Him. It is to be so sure of our divine Gardener, and of His skill and wisdom, that it will never cross our minds to question His plan of cultivation. It is to grow as the lilies grow, or as babies grow—without a care and without anxiety; to grow by an inner power that cannot help but grow; to grow because He who has planted us has planted a growing thing, and has made us to grow.

Surely this is what Jesus meant when He said, "Consider the lilies how they grow: they toil not, they spin not; and yet I say unto you, that Solomon in all his glory was not arrayed like one of these" (Luke 12:27). "Which of you with taking thought can add to his stature one cubit?" (Luke 12:25).

There is no effort in the growing of a child or of a lily. They don't stretch or strain, or make any sort of effort to grow; they aren't even conscious that they *are* growing. They grow by a power contained within, together with the nourishment and care provided by mother or gardener.

All our toiling and spinning to make for ourselves beautiful spiritual garments, all our stretching and straining to grow spiritually will accomplish nothing. No man by taking thought *can* add one cubit to his stature, physical or spiritual. And no spiritual garment of our own making can ever equal the beautiful dress with which God clothes the plants that grow in the soil of His grace.

If I could only make you realize how completely helpless we are in this matter of spiritual growth, you would find a large part of the strain taken out of your life. Imagine a child possessed with the idea that he won't grow unless he makes some personal effort to do so. He might rig up a combination of ropes and pulleys and spend years trying to stretch himself up to the desired height; but he would succeed only in exhausting himself. Equally ridiculous is the idea of a lily's trying to sew beautiful garments for itself.

Yet these two illustrations give only too accurate a picture of what many Christians are trying to do. Knowing they *ought* to grow and feeling an instinctive desire for growth, they try to accomplish it by toiling, spinning, stretching, straining, and engaging in such a round of self-effort that it is tiring just to think about it.

I am not trying to belittle the importance of growth, but to make you understand that the only effective way to grow is God's way. See to it that you are planted in grace, and then let God cultivate you in His own way and by His own means. Open yourself to the sunshine of His presence, and to the rain and the dew of heaven. Leaves, flowers, and fruit must surely come in their season; for the Lord is a skillful Gardener, and His harvest never fails.

But make certain that your life contains no barriers against God's sun and rain. The thinnest covering over a plant may serve to shield it from both, so that the plant withers even in the best soil. Just so, the slightest barrier between your soul and Christ may cause you to dwindle and fade, like a plant kept in a cellar or under a basket. Keep your life clear of every such barrier. Open up your whole being to receive every influence the Lord may bring to bear upon you. Bask in the sunshine of His love. Drink the waters of His goodness. Like a sunflower, keep your face turned toward Him.

I repeat: *You need make no effort to grow.* Concentrate your efforts on abiding in the Vine. The Vinedresser who cares for the Vine will care for its branches also. He will prune, water, and cultivate them so that they will grow and bring forth much fruit.

Perhaps it seems to you at the moment that you are planted in a desert, where nothing can grow. If you will put yourself totally into the hands of the Lord, He will make that desert "blossom as the rose" (Isaiah 35:1) and will cause the thirsty land to become "springs of water" (Isaiah 35:7). For the promise is sure:

> . . . the man who trusts in the Lord . . . .
> shall be like a tree planted by the waterside, that
> stretches its roots along the stream. When the
> heat comes it has nothing to fear; its spreading
> foliage stays green. In a year of drought it feels
> no care, and does not cease to bear fruit.
>
> Jeremiah 17:7, 8 NEB

The moment we put our growing into God's hands, He is able to turn any soil, whatever it may be like, into the soil of grace. He doesn't need to transplant us into a different field. Right where we are, He takes the very things that were our greatest hindrances and transforms them into the most effective means of our growth. No matter how bleak our circumstances, His wonder-working power can accomplish this transformation—*if* we trust Him with our lives and our growing.

Surely He can be trusted. Whether He sends storms, winds, rain, or sunshine, we must accept them all from His hands. Never doubt that He who has undertaken to culti- vate you, and to bring you to maturity, knows the very best way of accomplishing His end. The very elements are all at His disposal, and He regulates them expressly with a view to your most rapid growth.

If you will give up all your efforts to grow and will put yourself and your growth entirely into God's hands, you will find that no difficulties in your case can baffle Him. No dwarfing or deformity in your past development, no ap- parent dryness of your inward springs of life can mar the perfect work that He will accomplish in you, if you will only let Him have His way with you. We have scriptural authority for this:

> I will heal their faithlessness; I will love them freely, for my anger has turned from them. I will be as the dew to Israel; he shall blossom as the lily, he shall strike root as the poplar; his shoots shall spread out; his beauty shall be like the olive, and his fragrance like Lebanon. They shall return and dwell beneath my shadow, they shall flourish as a garden; they shall blossom as the vine, their fragrance shall be like the wine of Lebanon.
>
> Hosea 14:4–7 RSV

Fear not, you beasts of the field, for the pastures of the wilderness are green; the tree bears its fruit, the fig tree and vine give their full yield . . . . I will restore to you the years which the swarming locust has eaten . . . . You shall eat in plenty and be satisfied, and praise the name of the Lord your God, who has dealt wondrously with you . . . .

Joel 2:22, 25, 26 RSV

Let your mind dwell on the Lord's words—"Consider the lilies how they grow: they toil not, they spin not"—until their meaning opens up to you. The picture they give is of a life and a growth far different from the ordinary life and growth of Christians. It is a life of rest and a growth without effort; yet the results are glorious. Every believer who will become a lily in the garden of the Lord, and will grow as the lilies grow, will be given the same glorious array He has given them.

This sort of growth in grace is possible only to those who have entered into the life of full trust. It is a growth which leads to maturity and fruit bearing. If you ask such believers how they grow so rapidly and bear so much fruit, their answer will be that they are not concerned about their growing. In fact, they are hardly conscious that they do grow. They are not watching themselves but looking to Jesus. He has told His followers to abide in Him, and has promised that those who do shall bring forth much fruit (John 15:1–5). Therefore they are concerned only about the abiding, which is their part. They leave the cultivating, growing, training, and pruning to God.

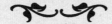

Let me close this chapter with a few practical words. We all know that physical growing is not a matter of effort, but the result of an inward life principle. All the stretching and pulling in the world won't make a dead oak grow. But a live oak grows even through a crack in the sidewalk. Obviously, then, the essential thing is to get within you the growing spiritual life; when you have that, you cannot help growing. And this life is the life "hid with Christ in God"—the wonderful life given by the indwelling Holy Spirit. If you are filled with this life, you can't help growing.

In this way, you must abide in Christ, the Vine, so that His life can flow through all your spiritual veins. Erect no barrier to His power. Yield yourself completely to Jesus and put your growing into His hands. Trust Him with it absolutely and always. Accept whatever comes to you each moment as being the sunshine or rain needed for that moment's growth. Say a continual *yes* to your Father's will.

Finally, in this, as in all the other concerns of your life:

> Have no anxiety about anything, but in everything by prayer and supplication with thanksgiving let your requests be made known to God. And the peace of God, which passes all understanding, will keep your hearts and your minds in Christ Jesus.
>
> Philippians 4:6 RSV

And what will be the result? You will experience a fulfillment of the promise:

The righteous flourish like the palm tree, and grow like a cedar in Lebanon. They are planted in the house of the Lord, they flourish in the courts of our God. They still bring forth fruit in old age, they are ever full of sap and green.

Psalms 92:12–14 RSV

15
Service

Of all the changes a believer experiences when he enters into the "life hid with Christ in God," probably the greatest is related to his Christian service. Too many people look upon the service they intend to do for the Lord as a kind of bondage. It is done solely as a matter of duty and is thought of as a trial or a "cross." Services which are initially undertaken with joy and delight soon become wearisome tasks. They are performed faithfully, perhaps, but not joyfully. The Christian finds himself saying, instead of the "May I?" of love, the "Must I?" of duty. The yoke that seemed so easy at first begins to gall, and the burden grows heavier rather than lighter.

One woman expressed it to me this way:

"When I was first converted, I was so full of joy and love that I was only too glad to do anything for my Lord. I took advantage of every opportunity to serve Him. But after a while, as the joy faded away, I began to wish I hadn't been quite so eager. Some of the tasks I had undertaken gradually became distasteful and burdensome. Since I had committed myself to them, I couldn't very well give them up—much as I wanted to.

"I was expected to visit the sick and pray with them; I was expected to speak at prayer meetings; I was expected to be always available for any sort of church work—and these expectations weighed heavily on me. Finally it became such a chore to live the sort of Christian life I had entered upon that I felt as if any kind of manual labor would be easier. I envied the women who had jobs in factories or who had to stay at home all day with young children."

Perhaps you know how this woman felt. Do you ever go about your work for the Lord as a slave goes to his daily task? You know you have to do it, because it is your duty;

but you can hardly wait to get back into your real interests and pleasures the moment your work is over. Of course you know it is wrong to feel this way and you are ashamed of yourself—but that doesn't help matters. You don't *love* your work; and if your conscience would let you, you would give it up altogether.

If this description doesn't fit your case, perhaps another one will. You *do* love your work in the abstract; but when it comes to doing it, you find so many problems connected with it and you are so unsure of your own ability that it becomes burdensome. Furthermore, you aren't always pleased with the results of your work, and you worry if they are not just what you would like.

The Christian who enters fully into the life of faith is delivered from all these problems. Service of any sort becomes delightful to him, because the Lord works in the fully surrendered will, ". . . inspiring both the will and the deed, for his own chosen purpose" (Philippians 2:13 NEB). Therefore the believer finds himself really *wanting* to do the things God wants him to do. It is always a pleasure to do the things we *want* to do, no matter how hard and physically tiring they may be.

Men who have gone almost literally to the ends of the earth in order to fulfill worldly ambitions seldom think of their travels as a "cross" they have to bear. Yet if the same sacrifice of home, friends, and worldly ease had been required of these men in the service of Christ, they would have felt that they were taking up crosses almost too heavy to be carried. It is the way we look at things that determines whether we think of them as crosses or as opportunities. I am saddened to think that so many Christians feel it is a burden to do for Christ something which a worldly man would gladly do for money.

What the world needs is more believers who *want* to do God's will as much as unbelievers want to do their own will. And this is what God intended for us and what He has promised us. The new covenant described in Hebrews 8:6–13 is different from the old covenant made on Sinai. That was a law given from the outside, controlling a man by force. The new covenant is a law written *within*, constraining a man by love.

God says, "I will put my laws into their mind, and write them in their hearts" (Hebrews 8:10). These words mean that we will *love* His laws; for we are bound to love anything written in our hearts. And if God puts His laws into our minds, we will obey His commands because we *want* to do what He wants us to—not because it is our duty to do so. In other words, God will be working in us "inspiring both the will and the deed."

No more effective plan than this could ever be conceived. I have often thought, in dealing with my own children, "Oh, if I could just get inside them and make them want to do what I want! It would be so easy to manage them then!" I have also learned from practical experience that the way to deal with cross-grained people is carefully to avoid suggesting my wishes to them. Instead, I try to induce *them* to suggest those same ideas. We are by nature a stiff-necked people, and we always tend to rebel against a law imposed on us from the outside. If the "law" seems to be our own idea, however, we obey it gladly.

God's plan, therefore, is to get inside the believer, so as to take over the control of his will and manage it for him. Then obedience is easy, and service becomes perfect freedom.

If you feel that you are under bondage in your service for God, you need to put your will completely into His hands. Surrender to Him the entire control of it and trust Him to bring all your wishes and pleasures into conformity with His own will. I have seen Him do this time after time, in cases where I would have thought it utterly impossible.

I know one woman who for years had been rebelling against doing something which she knew was her duty but which she hated to do. Finally, out of the depths of her despair, she gave her will in that matter into the hands of God and began to say to Him, "Thy will be done; *Thy will be done!*" Within an hour, the thing she had hated so much began to look desirable to her.

It is wonderful to see what miracles God can work in wills that are completely surrendered to Him. He makes hard things easy and bitter things sweet. It isn't that He puts an easy thing in the place of the hard one; He actually *changes* the hard thing into an easy one. And this is salvation. Do try it, if you are performing your daily Christian service as a hard and weary task. See if Jesus won't transform the life of bondage you are now living into a life of delightful freedom.

If you are one of those who love His will in the abstract but find the doing of it hard and burdensome, you too will find deliverance in the life of faith. In this life no burdens are carried, no anxieties felt. The Lord is our Burden-bearer, and He wants us to lay every care on Him. Through the Apostle Paul, He says that we are to have no anxiety about *anything*—not even about our service; but we are to make our requests known to Him and let Him take care of them (Philippians 4:6).

Why should we worry about whether we are fit? The

Master Workman surely has a right to use any tool He pleases for His work, and it is plainly not the business of the tool to decide whether it is the right one. *He* knows—and if He chooses to use us, we can be sure we are fit. If we only knew it, our fitness lies chiefly in our utter helplessness. His strength can be made perfect only in our weakness (2 Corinthians 12:9).

I saw a perfect illustration of this truth when I visited an institution for retarded children and watched them exercising with dumbbells. Most of the children were physically strong, but they all lacked coordination. Consequently, they made many awkward movements. Now and then one of the children made the right movement at the right time; but when this happened, it was purely accidental.

One little girl, however, *consistently* made perfect movements in rhythm with the music. This wasn't because she had more strength than the others, but *because she had no strength at all.* She couldn't even grasp the dumbbells, much less lift them. Therefore, the teacher had to stand behind her and do it all for her. He knew exactly how to perform those exercises, for he himself had planned them. Therefore when he did them, they were done right. She did nothing but give her arms entirely into his hands, and he did the rest. The yielding was her part; the work was all his. Her utter weakness was her greatest strength.

If this is a picture of our Christian life, no wonder Paul could say, "Most gladly therefore will I . . . *glory* in my infirmities, that the power of Christ may rest upon me" (2 Corinthians 12:9). Who would not glory in being so utterly weak and helpless that the power of Jesus would be able to work in him without hindrance?

If the work is the Lord's, the responsibility for the outcome is His also, and we have nothing left to worry about. He knows everything there is to know about it, and He can manage it all. In that case, why not leave it all with Him and consent to let Him treat us like children and show us just where to go and what to do?

The most effective workers I know are those who don't allow themselves a moment's anxiety about their work. They commit it all to Jesus, asking Him to guide them step by step and trusting Him implicitly to provide the wisdom and strength they need for each day's work. To see them, you might almost think that they are *too* free from care, where such important matters are at stake. But when you have learned God's secret of trusting, you will see that a life yielded up to His working is one of rest as well as power.

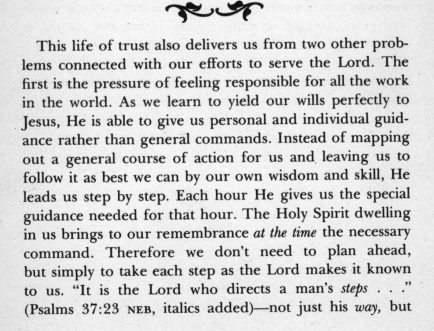

This life of trust also delivers us from two other problems connected with our efforts to serve the Lord. The first is the pressure of feeling responsible for all the work in the world. As we learn to yield our wills perfectly to Jesus, He is able to give us personal and individual guidance rather than general commands. Instead of mapping out a general course of action for us and leaving us to follow it as best we can by our own wisdom and skill, He leads us step by step. Each hour He gives us the special guidance needed for that hour. The Holy Spirit dwelling in us brings to our remembrance *at the time* the necessary command. Therefore we don't need to plan ahead, but simply to take each step as the Lord makes it known to us. "It is the Lord who directs a man's *steps* . . ." (Psalms 37:23 NEB, italics added)—not just his *way,* but each separate step in that way.

Many Christians make the mistake of expecting to receive God's commands to them all at once. If He tells them, for instance, to give a tract to one person in a waiting room, they think He wants them to give tracts to everybody they see. In that way they burden themselves with an impossible task.

Linda is a young Christian who was sent by the Lord to speak a message to one person whom she met in a walk. She took this instruction as a general command and thought she must speak to everyone she met about his soul. Soon she was so overcome by this enormous responsibility that she became afraid to go outside her own house for fear of meeting someone and having to witness to him.

Finally Linda shared her problem with Howard, an older Christian who had had more experience in the ways of God with His servants. He told her that she was making a mistake: that the Lord has His own special task for each servant of His and doesn't intend for any of His workers to feel responsible for doing everything—any more than the president of a well-run business expects any one employee to take upon himself the work of all the others. Howard told Linda just to put herself under the Lord's personal guidance and trust Him to point out to her each particular person He wanted her to speak to.

Linda followed this advice and laid the burden of her witnessing on the Lord. As a result, she was able to carry on a great work for Him without stress or strain.

Putting ourselves into God's hands might be compared to connecting a machine to a steam engine. The power is not in the machine but in the steam. Disconnected from the power source, the machinery is perfectly useless. But once the connection is made, the machine works without effort because of the mighty power behind it. In the same way, the Christian life becomes easy and natural when it is motivated and empowered by the divine life within.

Most Christians live under a strain, simply because their wills are not *fully* in harmony with the will of God. The connection is not perfectly made at every point, and effort is required to make the machine function. Once the connection is fully made, the Holy Spirit can work within them, furnishing the faith and power to move mountains.

The life of faith delivers us from another problem in serving—the after-reflections which normally follow any endeavor. These after-reflections are of two sorts. Sometimes we congratulate ourselves upon our success and are lifted up; at other times, we are depressed over our failure. Of the two, I think the first is more dangerous, although the latter, of course, is more painful. In the life of trust, however, neither will trouble us. Having committed our work to the Lord, we are satisfied to leave the outcome to Him.

Years ago I came across this sentence in an old book:

> At the close of an action, never indulge in any reflection of any kind, whether self-congratulation or despair. Forget the things that are behind the moment they are past, leaving them with God.

This advice has been of great value to me. When I am tempted to indulge in after-reflections of either sort, I reject the temptation at once and positively refuse to think about my work at all. I simply trust the Lord to overrule my mistakes and to bless the work as He chooses.

To sum up what is needed for happy and effective service: Simply put your work into the Lord's hands and leave it there. Take it to Him in prayer and ask Him to guide you, give you wisdom, and make the necessary arrangements. Then, when you arise from your knees, don't take the burden back and try to make your own arrangements. Leave it with the Lord, and remember that you mustn't feel anxious about what you've entrusted to Him. Trust and worry simply don't go together.

If your work is a burden, it is because you aren't trusting it to Him. If you do trust it to Him, you will find that the yoke He puts upon you is easy and the burden He gives you to carry is light. Even in the midst of a life of ceaseless activity, you will find rest for your soul.

If Jesus only had a band of such helpless, trusting workers, there is no limit to what He could do through them. May God raise up such an army speedily! I urge you to enlist in it and to ". . . yield your bodies to him as implements for doing right" (Romans 6:13 NEB), to be used by Him as He pleases.

16
Practical Results in Daily Life

If there is truth in all I have said about the life of faith, the results should be plainly evident in the behavior of the people who have entered into this life. They should be truly ". . . a pure people marked out for his own, eager to do good" (Titus 2:14 NEB).

The world may never read the Bible, but it will read our lives; and these can be, as Paul said, letters from Christ, "known and read by all men" (*see* 2 Corinthians 3:3, 2 RSV). Unless, however, our lives present clear evidence of being transformed by the power of Christ, the world will reject the God we claim to believe in.

In this chapter, therefore, I want to write about the *fruits* of the life of faith, and to emphasize our responsibility to ". . . live lives worthy of [our] high calling" (Ephesians 4:1 PHILLIPS). May I speak to you as friend to friend, and speak very plainly?

The usual standard of Christian living is so low that the least sign of obvious consecration is looked upon with surprise, and often with disapproval, by many church members. Most Christians are satisfied with lives so conformed to the world that a casual observer can see no difference between them and their non-Christian neighbors. But those who have heard God calling them to a life of consecration and trust must come out from the world and be separate.

In the words of Jesus and in the letters of the Apostles Paul and Peter, we find principles of conduct laid down for the followers of Christ. If all Christians observed them, the church would indeed be "the salt of the earth" and "the light of the world" (Matthew 5:13, 14). Here are just a few of these guidelines:

179

1. We must let our minds dwell on heavenly things and not on earthly ones (Colossians 3:2).
2. We must seek "first the kingdom of God, and his righteousness" (Matthew 6:33), surrendering everything that would interfere with this single-minded search.
3. We must have the mind that was in Christ Jesus (Philippians 2:5).
4. "As aliens in a foreign land," we must "abstain from the lusts of the flesh which are at war with the soul" (*see* 1 Peter 2:11 NEB).
5. We must abstain even from the *appearance* of evil (1 Thessalonians 5:22).
6. We must "be kind to one another, tenderhearted, forgiving one another, as God in Christ forgave [us]" (Ephesians 4:32 RSV).
7. We must not resent injuries or unkindness, but must return good for evil and turn the other cheek to the hand that strikes us (Luke 6:27–29).
8. We must always take the lowest place among our fellowmen (Luke 14:10) and must seek the honor of others rather than our own honor (Romans 12:10). In other words, we must be gentle, meek, and yielding, not standing up for our own rights but standing up for the rights of others.
9. We must do all that we do for the glory of God (1 Corinthians 10:31).

To sum up, we must be holy in all our behavior, because "the One who called [us] is holy . . ." and "because Scripture says, 'You shall be holy, for I am holy' " (1 Peter 1:15, 16 NEB).

These very practical rules of conduct call for a life totally different from the lives of most Christians. They call for us to turn our backs on *everything* that is contrary to the perfect will of God. Following these guidelines will make us indeed "a peculiar people" (1 Peter 2:9; Titus 2:14), not only in the eyes of God but in the eyes of the world. Wherever we go, our conduct and our conversation will reveal that we are followers of Jesus and, like Him, are not of the world (John 17:14).

No longer will we feel that our money is ours. It is the Lord's, to be used in His service. No longer are we at liberty to use our energies exclusively in the pursuit of personal happiness and worldly gain. We are forbidden to seek the highest places or to strain after worldly advantages. We are no longer permitted to make self the center of all our thoughts and all our efforts. Our days will be spent in serving the Lord, not ourselves. We will be called upon to "bear one another's burdens . . ." (Galatians 6:2 RSV). And all our daily tasks will be performed more conscientiously than ever before, because we will be doing them ". . . not merely with an outward show of service, to curry favour with men, but with single-mindedness, out of reverence for the Lord" (Colossians 3:22 NEB).

You may be wondering why all these rules of conduct are necessary, when I have been saying all along that our only responsibility is to trust God and yield our wills totally to Him. If we do this, won't the Holy Spirit lead us to do the right thing in every situation?

The answer is that He surely will *if* we have given ourselves up to His guidance and *if* we are able to recognize that guidance. But unless the right standards of Christian life are set before us, our ignorance may keep us from hearing His voice. For that reason, I have been practical and specific about what those standards are.

When a consecrated believer follows the Lord faithfully, several evidences appear sooner or later. Meekness and quietness of spirit become, in time, the characteristics of daily life. Other outward signs of the life that is "hid with Christ in God" are (1) grateful acceptance of the will of God as it comes in the hourly events of each day; (2) pliability in the hands of God to do or to bear whatever He assigns us; (3) a sweet disposition, even under provocation; (4) calmness in the midst of turmoil and confusion; (5) willingness to let others have their way; (6) refusal to notice slights and affronts; (7) absence of worry, anxiety, and fear.

As Christians lay aside their selfish concerns and become more considerate of others, their habits also change. They begin to dress and live in simple, healthful ways and to give up self-indulgent habits such as smoking and drinking. As more and more time is given to helping others, useless occupations gradually drop out of the life. God's glory and the welfare of His creatures become the Christian's absorbing delight. The voice is dedicated to Him, to be used in singing His praises. The purse is placed at His disposal. The pen is dedicated to write for Him; the lips, to speak for Him; the hands and the feet, to do His bidding. Year after year such Christians grow more unworldly, more like Christ. Finally their faces express so much of the divine life within them that it is obvious to everyone who looks at them that they live with Jesus.

If you have read this far, you have had at least some intimations of the life I am describing. Have you begun to feel dimly conscious of the voice of God speaking to you about these things? Has it disturbed you to realize how selfish your life is? Has your conscience been troubled about some of your habits and pastimes? Have you begun to wish that you could change some of them? Do you feel a yearning for a life of deeper devotion and greater service?

All these longings and doubts are the voice of the Holy Spirit in your heart, calling you to give up everything that is contrary to His will. I beg you not to turn away from Him! If you only knew what wonderful blessings He has in store for those who are obedient to His voice, you would eagerly and joyfully yield to every one of His requirements.

The heights of Christian perfection and joy can be reached only by faithfully following the Holy Spirit as He reveals the way to you, one step at a time, in the little things of your daily life. If there is anything in your life that you feel doubtful or troubled about, surrender it at once to the Lord, thanking Him for His guidance. Be perfectly pliable in His hands: go where He leads you, turn away from everything that troubles your conscience. If you obey Him perfectly, He will lead you swiftly and easily into a life so Christlike that it will be a testimony to everyone around you—a far greater testimony than you will ever realize.

Anne is a Christian who, in the depths of darkness and despair, consecrated herself to Jesus and made up her mind to follow Him wherever He might lead her. Immediately after she made this surrender of the will, the Holy Spirit began to speak to her, suggesting little acts of service, troubling her about certain habits in her life, showing her where she was selfish and un-Christlike. She recognized His voice and gave up all the practices He asked her to. Her progress was rapid, and day by day she became conformed more and more to His will. Her life was such a testimony to those around her that some who had been opposed to her "fanatical devotion" were persuaded to make a similar surrender.

After Anne had been following Him in this way for just three months, Jesus was able to reveal to her some of the deepest secrets of His love and to baptize her with the Holy Spirit.

Do you think Anne has ever regretted her decision to follow Jesus wholeheartedly, or that she feels anything but gratitude and joy when she reviews the steps—some of them hard to take at the time—by which He led her to this wonderful experience? If you are longing for the same blessing, give yourself up, as Anne did, to the guidance of the Holy Spirit, and don't shrink from any surrender He may ask you to make.

Surely you know that you can trust Him! If He asks you to do—or stop doing—some things that seem insignificant, remember that His viewpoint is different from man's. Things that look small to you may be seen by Him as the key and the clue to your complete surrender. In order to mold you into conformity to His will, He must have you pliable in His hands, and yielding in the little things is often the secret to achieving this pliability.

Your one great desire is to follow Him fully. Then can't you say a continual yes to all His commands, whether small or large, and trust Him to lead you by the shortest road to the place He wants you to be? Whether you knew it or not, this is what your consecration meant. It meant *inevitable obedience.* It meant that the will of God was, from then on, to be your will—under all circumstances and at all times. It meant that from that moment you surrendered your freedom of choice and gave yourself completely into the control of your Lord. It meant following Him hour by hour wherever He might lead you, with no turning back.

And now I urge you to make good your promise. Let everything else go, so that you will be able to live out, in a practical way, the Christ life that dwells within you. You are united to Jesus by a wonderful tie; walk, then, as He walked, and show the unbelieving world the reality of His presence. Don't be afraid to agree to this, because He is your Savior and His power will do it all for you. He is not asking you, in your weakness, to do it yourself. He only asks you to yield yourself to Him and let Him work in you "to will and to do" by His own mighty power. Your part is to yield; His part is to work. Never will He give you any command without giving you the power to obey it.

In this matter, "take no thought for the morrow" (Matthew 6:34), but give yourself generously and trustingly to Jesus. He has promised never to put His sheep forth into any path without Himself going before them to make the way easy and safe (John 10:4). Take each little step as He makes it plain to you. Bring all your life to Him and ask Him to regulate and guide each of its details. Follow gladly and promptly all the suggestions of His Holy Spirit.

Day by day you will find Him bringing you into greater conformity with His will in all things. He is making you, as fast as you are able to bear it, into "a vessel for noble use, consecrated and useful to [Him], ready for any good work" (*see* 2 Timothy 2:21 RSV). When He has finished His work, you will have the joy of being a "letter from Christ, known and read by all men" (*see* 2 Corinthians 3:3, 2 RSV). Your light will shine so brightly that men, seeing the *good* you do (not *you*), will give praise, not to you, but to your Father in heaven (*see* Matthew 5:16 NEB).

17

The Joy of Obedience

I have told you about some of the difficulties in this life of faith. Now let me tell you about some of its joys. One of the greatest of these is the joy of obedience.

A long time ago, I read this sentence somewhere:

Perfect obedience would be perfect happiness, if only we had perfect confidence in the power we were obeying.

It struck me as suggesting a way of happiness I had never dreamed of, and gave me the vision of a life that would satisfy all my longings. This life has now been revealed to me as a reality; for I have found in Jesus the One whom I can obey with perfect confidence.

If Jesus has revealed Himself to you and asked for your complete surrender, you don't know the joy you are missing by holding back. Perhaps you are willing to make a partial surrender, and think it is fitting and proper to do so. But *complete* surrender, with nothing held back, seems too much to ask. You are afraid of it; you think it is too great a risk. *Measurable* obedience appeals to you; *perfect* obedience appalls you.

For one thing, you see some Christians whose consciences don't seem to bother them when they do things that you know Jesus doesn't want you to do. Or perhaps you see them *not* doing things that you know He does want you to do. In either case, it seems hard that they should have so much more freedom than you do.

Though you don't yet know it, this very difference between you and them is your privilege. Jesus said, "The man who has received my commands and obeys them—he it is who loves me; and he who loves me will be loved by my

189

Father; and I will love him and disclose myself to him"
(John 14:21 NEB).

You *have* His commandments; those whom you envy
don't have them. *You* know His will concerning many
things about which *they* are still in the dark. Isn't this a
privilege rather than a cause for regret? Jesus is able to tell
you things He doesn't reveal to those who are further off.
Don't you realize what a degree of closeness this implies?

There are many relationships in life which require only
moderate degrees of devotion. We can have really pleasant
friendships with people whose interests and way of life are
quite different from ours. We enjoy their company when
we are with them, but separation from them doesn't distress us. We feel free to form other, more intimate friendships. The affection between us isn't great enough to give
us either the privilege or the desire to share each other's
most private affairs. A certain degree of reserve and distance is suitable in such friendships.

When friendship becomes love, however, all this is
changed. Then a union of personalities takes place which
makes everything that is of interest to one become interesting to the other. Separate ways of life are no longer possible. The reserve and distance suitable to mere friendship is
fatal in love. Love gives everything and must have everything in return. The wishes of the beloved become binding
obligations to the lover.

Does a lover envy the cool, calm, reasonable friendships
that others have? Does he regret the obligations created by
his devotion to his beloved? Or does he glory in these
obligations and pity everyone who is not in love?

If you have ever known this sort of earthly relationship—if you have ever loved a person enough to find joy in

making sacrifices for that person—then I beg you to give Jesus this kind of love. He Himself is longing for you to do so.

He loves you with more than the love of friendship. He loves you the way a bridegroom loves his bride, and nothing but total surrender will satisfy Him. He has given you all of Himself, and He asks for all of you in return. For you to hold back anything will grieve Him to the heart. For your sake He poured out all He had, and for His sake you must do the same.

Be generous in your surrender! Meet His measureless devotion for you with a measureless devotion to Him. Be glad and eager to hand over the control of your life to Him. Whatever there is of you, let Him have it all. Give up forever everything that separates you from Him. From this time on, give up even your freedom of choice.

Haven't you sometimes longed to lavish your love on someone who was hardly aware of your existence? Haven't you felt such a desire for self-surrender and devotion that it seemed to burn like a fire within you, because there was no person to whom you dared give it? If so, why do you shrink back when you hear Jesus calling you into a place of nearness to Him—nearness which will require separation from everything else and will make this sort of devotion not only possible but necessary?

Does it seem hard that Jesus reveals more of His mind to you than He does to others, and that He won't let you be happy in anything that separates you from Him? Do you *want* to go where He can't go with you, or to have interests that He can't share?

Surely your answer is *no!* Surely you will rejoice to do His will, and surely it would break your heart to disobey even His slightest wish. The very narrowness of the path He marks out for you is a cause for rejoicing. The obligations of love will become its privileges; and your right to lavish everything you have upon your Lord will give you a new understanding of joy. The perfect happiness of perfect obedience will dawn upon you, and you will begin to know what Jesus meant when He said, "I *delight* to do thy will, O my God . . ." (Psalms 40:8).

And do you think the joy will be all on your side? The Scriptures, especially the Song of Solomon, give us glimpses of the delight our Lord has in those who have surrendered themselves to Him and who love to obey Him. That *we* should need Him is easy to understand; that *He* should need us seems incomprehensible. Yet He says it, and we must believe Him.

He has made our hearts capable of this supreme affection, and has offered Himself as the object of it. It is infinitely precious to Him. He longs for it and seeks it from His people. He is continually knocking at every heart (Revelation 3:20), asking to be taken in as the supreme object of love.

Jesus says to the believer, "Will you accept Me as your Beloved? Are you willing to follow Me into suffering and loneliness, and endure hardness for My sake, and to ask no reward but My smile of approval and My word of praise? Will you give Me absolute control of your life? Will you be content with pleasing Me and Me only? May I have My way with you in all things? Will you come into so close a union with Me as to make a separation from the world necessary? Will you accept Me as your Bridegroom and leave all others to cleave only to Me?"

He makes this offer of union with Himself to every believer. But not all say yes to Him. Some feel that their other loves and other interests are too precious to be cast aside. Although they don't miss heaven because of this decision, they miss an unspeakable present joy.

I hope you are not one of these. I pray that you have responded eagerly and gladly to all His offers, "Yes, Lord, yes!" If so, you are ready to pour out upon Him all your love and devotion. The enthusiasm of your self-surrender may disturb more prudent Christians, who can't even conceive of such a separation from the world as your love for Jesus makes necessary. The sacrifices and services which are possible and sweet to you can't even be comprehended by these "moderate" believers.

The love life upon which you have entered gives you the right to pour out your *all* upon your Beloved. Freedoms which less committed Christians don't dare take are not only your privilege but your duty. Jesus claims from you, because of your union with Him, far more than He claims from them. What is lawful to them, love has made unlawful for you. He tells you His secrets and expects from you an instant response to every requirement of His love.

You have entered upon a glorious, unspeakable privilege! What does it matter to you if men hate you, separate you from their company, and reproach you for the sake of Jesus? You may well "rejoice in that day, and leap for joy, for . . . your reward is great in heaven . . ." (Luke 6:23 RSV). If you share His suffering, you will also share His glory (1 Peter 4:13).

Your love and devotion are Jesus' reward for all He has done for you, and they are unspeakably sweet to Him.

Don't be afraid to give yourself wholeheartedly and without reservation to your Lord. Others may not approve, but He will—and that is enough.

Let Him have all there is of you: body, soul, spirit, time, talents, voice—everything. Lay your whole life open before Him and ask Him to control it. Say to Him each day, "Lord, how shall I spend this day so as to please You? Where shall I go? What shall I do? Whom shall I visit? What shall I say?" Give Him control of your appearance and say, "Lord, tell me how to dress so as to please You." Give Him your reading, your occupations, your friendships, and say, "Lord, speak to me about all these and tell me just what You want me to do about them all." Don't let a day or even an hour go by when you are not *consciously* doing His will and following Him wholly. This personal service to Him will give a glow to your life that will brighten the most monotonous existence.

Have you ever grieved for the lost romance of your youth? Bring Christ into all the details of your life and you will find a far grander romance than youth could ever know. Furthermore, nothing will seem hard or stern again—not even the drabbest existence or the most menial tasks. Any life lived in Christ and *with* Christ—a life that follows Him wherever He may lead—will be filled with a spiritual romance that will make every hour glorious.

18
Divine Union

All the dealings of God with His children have one purpose: to bring them into oneness with Himself, that the prayer of Jesus may be fulfilled:

> That they may all be one; even as thou, Father, art in me, and I in thee, that they also may be in us, so that the world may believe that thou hast sent me . . . . I in them and thou in me, that they may become perfectly one, so that the world may know that thou hast sent me and hast loved them even as thou hast loved me.
>
> John 17:21, 23 RSV

This union with Him was God's purpose for His people before the foundation of the world (Ephesians 1:9, 10), and it was accomplished in the death of Christ. Such a union has been proclaimed by the Scriptures and is realized as an actual experience by many of God's children.

By many, but not by all. It is possible for all, and God has not hidden it or made it hard; but because of unbelief or lack of understanding, many fail to grasp it. Right now the Lord is calling believers everywhere to surrender themselves to Him, so that they can be brought into the personal realization of union with Him.

All the previous steps in the Christian life lead up to this union. The Lord has made us for it. Until we have understood it and voluntarily consented to enter into it, He is not satisfied and we have not found the rest intended for us.

The history of the disciples gives a picture of the usual Christian experience. First they were brought to a realization of their need, and they came to Christ and gave Him their allegiance. Then they followed Him, worked for Him, and believed in Him; yet how unlike Him they were! We see them arguing over who would be first in the King-

197

dom, misunderstanding Jesus' mission and His words, forsaking Him in the time of danger. Imperfect as they were, however, He still sent them out to preach, recognized them as His disciples, and gave them power to work for Him. They knew Christ only "after the flesh" (2 Corinthians 5:16), as outside of them—their Lord, but not yet their Life.

Then these same disciples experienced Pentecost and came to know Jesus as inwardly revealed, as one with them in actual union—their very indwelling life. From then on He was to them Christ within, working in them to inspire ". . . both the will and the deed, for his own chosen purpose" (Philippians 2:13 NEB), delivering them from bondage to the law of sin and death (Romans 8:2). No longer was there a war of wills between themselves and Him. One will alone animated them, and that was His. They were made *one* with Him.

Surely you can see your own Christian experience in the disciples' history, though perhaps you have not yet reached the final stage of it. You may have left much to follow Christ. You may have believed in Him, worked for Him, and loved Him—and yet may not be like Him. You have given Him your allegiance and your confidence, but you have not yet experienced union with Him. There are two wills, two interests, two lives. You have not yet lost your own life that you may live only in His.

Once it was you and not Christ. Then it was you and Christ. Perhaps now it is Christ and you. But has it come to be Christ only, and not you at all?

If not, let me tell you how to take the final step of faith that will lead you out of self and into Christ. If you truly desire to abide in Him forever and to know no life but His, you need only to understand what the Bible teaches about this marvelous union, so that you can be sure it is really intended for you.

Start by reading 1 Corinthians 3:16: "Do you not know that you are God's temple and that God's Spirit dwells in you?" (RSV). Then look at the opening of the chapter and see that these wonderful words were spoken to babes in Christ who still lived "on the purely human level of [their] lower nature" (*see* 1 Corinthians 3:3 NEB). This union of which I speak, this unspeakable mystery of an indwelling God, belongs to even the weakest believer. So you don't need to ask for something new, but only to claim what you already have. It is absolutely true of every believer that his "body is a temple of the Holy Spirit within [him], which [he has] from God" (*see* 1 Corinthians 6:19 RSV).

Unless the believer knows this scriptural promise, however, and lives in the power of it, it might as well not be true. The treasure buried in a field is just as real before it is discovered as afterward, but it is of no benefit to the owner of the field until he finds it and uses it. So it is with the life of Christ in each believer. It has been present ever since he accepted Jesus as his Savior, but its power is not available to him until he consciously and voluntarily gives up his own life and accepts Christ's life in its place.

∼✦∽

Here is the way I see it. I imagine Christ shut up in some remote room of a house, unknown and unnoticed by the people who live there. He longs to make Himself known to them, to take part in their daily lives and share in all their interests—but He is unwilling to force Himself upon them. Nothing but a voluntary invitation to companionship can satisfy the needs of His love.

Days and years pass by, during which that favored family remains in ignorance of His presence. They come and go about their daily affairs with no idea that they have such a wonderful guest. Since they make their plans without reference to Him, His wisdom to guide and His strength to protect are lost to them. When sorrow comes, the family spends days and weeks in lonely sadness—days which might have been gladdened by His presence.

Then suddenly the announcement is made: "The Lord is in the house!"

How will its owner receive the news? Will he thankfully open up every door for Jesus to enter in? Or will he be frightened by His presence and try to hide in some private corner to avoid his Guest's all-seeing eye?

I make the glad announcement to you today that the Lord is in your heart. Since the day of your conversion He has been living there, but you have been unaware of His presence. Because you didn't know He was there and haven't looked for Him, your life has been lonely and full of failure.

Now that you know Jesus is living in your heart, how will you receive Him? Are you glad to have Him? Will you open every door of your life to welcome Him in? Will you joyfully and thankfully give Him control of your life? Will you consult Him about everything, and let Him decide each step you take and mark out every path for you to walk in? Will you invite Him into your innermost being and ask Him to share your most hidden life? Will you say yes to His longing for union with you, and eagerly hand yourself and all your concerns over into His hands? If so, then you will begin to know something of the joy of union with Christ.

Yet this analogy, after all, gives only a faint suggestion of the marvelous reality. To be brought into actual union with Jesus is far more glorious than merely to have Him as a guest in your home or in your heart. To be one with

Him—to have one will, one purpose, one interest, one life—human words can't express the glory of this. Yet I so much want to express it! I want to make you so hungry to realize this union that you cannot rest without it.

Do you understand the words, *one with Christ?* Do you catch a glimpse of their marvelous meaning and of their reality? Try to picture this reality. Think what it means to have no life but His life, no will but His will, no interests but His interests; to share His riches, to enter into His joys and His sorrows, to manifest His life, to have the same mind as He did, to think and feel and act and walk as He did!

Will you accept this life? Jesus won't force it on you. He wants you as His companion and His friend, and a forced union would be incompatible with this relationship. It must be voluntary on your part. The bride must say a willing *yes* to her bridegroom, or their union brings no joy. Can you say a willing *yes* to your Lord?

It is such a simple transaction, and yet so real! Only three steps are required.

1. Be convinced that the Scriptures teach this indwelling of the Lord.
2. Surrender your whole being to Him, to be possessed by Him.
3. *Believe* that He has taken possession and is dwelling in you. Begin to consider yourself dead, and to think of Jesus as your only life. Hold onto this attitude by saying over and over, "I have been crucified with Christ: the life I now live is not my life, but the life which Christ lives in me . . ." (Galatians 2:20 NEB). Say it day and night, until it becomes as habitual as breathing.

By faith, continually put off your self-life and put on the life of Christ (Galatians 3:27; Romans 13:14). Repeat this act until it becomes the attitude of your whole being. If you do this day after day, you will find that His life will be revealed in your mortal body (*see* 2 Corinthians 4:11 NEB). You will learn the full meaning of salvation and will have your eyes opened to secrets of the Lord that you had never dreamed of.

Paul has compared the union between Christ and the church to the marriage relationship. Quoting the words of Jesus, ". . . 'a man shall leave his father and mother and shall be joined to his wife, and the two shall become one flesh,' " Paul says, "It is a great truth that is hidden here. I for my part refer it to Christ and to the church" (Ephesians 5:31, 32 NEB). In the same chapter, Paul tells us that Christ "provides and cares for" the church, "because it is his body, of which we are living parts" (*see* Ephesians 5:29, 30 NEB).

What is your response to all this? What can you do but receive it fully, with all its tremendous possibilities for love and union between you and Jesus? Receive Him as your bridegroom, and seek all the manifestations of His love. Let Him bring you to the banqueting house, and let His banner over you be love (Song of Solomon 2:4).

When you have experienced this glorious union, you will know at last what Jesus meant when He said:

> The glory which thou hast given me I have given to them, that they may be one even as we are one, I in them and thou in me, that they may become perfectly one, so that the world may know that thou hast sent me and hast loved them even as thou hast loved me.
>
> John 17:22, 23 RSV

19
The Chariots of God

It was a wise person who said, "Earthly cares are a heavenly discipline." But they can be even more than that—they can be God's chariots, sent to take the believer to new heights of spiritual victory.

True, they don't *look* like chariots. They look like sufferings, trials, defeats, misunderstandings, disappointments, even tragedies. They look like steamrollers of misery and wretchedness, designed to crush us into the earth. The steamroller is the visible thing; the chariot of God is the invisible.

The king of Syria came against Elisha with horses and chariots that could be seen by every eye; but God had chariots that could be seen only by the eye of faith. Elisha's servant, sighting the visible army, was dismayed, as most of us would have been. ". . . We are doomed, sir!" he cried. "What shall we do?" (2 Kings 6:15 TEV). But the prophet, whose eyes were opened to see the invisible army of God, sat calmly within his house. His prayer for his servant was, "O Lord, open his eyes and let him see!" (*see* 2 Kings 6:17 TEV).

This is the prayer we need to make for ourselves and for one another. The world all around us is full of God's horses and chariots, waiting to carry us to victory. When our spiritual eyes have been opened, we will be able to see in all the events of life—whether large or small, joyful or sad—a "chariot" for our souls.

Everything that comes to us becomes a chariot of God the minute we treat it as such. On the other hand, even the smallest trial may be a steamroller to crush us into despair if we see it in that way. It is up to us to choose which it will be. The deciding factor is not the events themselves, but the way we take them. If we lie down under them and let them roll over us, they become crushing steamrollers; but if we willingly climb into them, they become God's chariots that will carry us to victory.

Elijah was taken up to heaven in a chariot of fire (2 Kings 2:11). Spiritually, the same thing happens to us whenever we enter one of God's chariots. We are taken not into the heaven above us, as Elijah was, but into the heaven within us. We are carried away from the low, earthly level, where pain and unhappiness are our lot, up into the "heavenly places in Christ" (Ephesians 1:3), where we can ride in triumph over all our hurts and disappointments.

These heavenly places, and the road that leads to them, are interior, not exterior. But the chariot that carries the soul over this road is generally some exterior event—some loss, trial, or disappointment. Like all chastening or discipline, it ". . . isn't enjoyable while it is happening—it hurts! But afterwards we can see the result, a quiet growth in grace and character" (Hebrews 12:11 LB).

No matter how severe God's discipline may seem at the present, look upon it as a chariot sent to carry your soul to new heights of spiritual growth.

The Bible tells us that, when God went forth to bring victory to His people, the storm cloud was His chariot (*see* Habakkuk 3:8 TEV). The clouds and storms that darken your skies and seem to come between you and God are only His chariots. Climb into them and ride victoriously with Him over all the darkness.

I once knew a minister who had a very slow secretary. She was a fine woman and was a great asset to the church, but her slowness was a constant source of irritation to this man. Every time he lost his temper with her, he was ashamed of himself and resolved to do better—but his resolutions were in vain. His life was made miserable by the conflict. One day it occurred to him that he had been praying for patience and that his secretary might have been sent by the Lord in answer to that prayer. From that time on, he accepted her slowness as a "chariot" to carry him to a victory over impatience. In time that victory was won, and he was never again disturbed by anyone's lack of speed.

At a convention of churchwomen, my friend Sarah was given a room with two other delegates. The first night of the meeting she wanted to sleep, but they wanted to talk. Their lack of consideration annoyed her so much that she lay awake fretting and fuming long after the others were quiet.

The next day, one of the speakers talked about God's chariots. That night, accepting her talkative roommates as a chariot to carry her into serenity, Sarah remained peaceful and calm. About midnight, however, when she knew they all ought to be sleeping, she said quietly, "Friends, I am lying here riding in a chariot." Instantly, perfect quiet reigned! Her chariot had at last carried her to outward as well as inward victory.

When we choose to ride in God's chariot instead of our own, victory is always ours. Our constant temptation is to trust in earthly resources. We can *see* them; they are tangible and look substantial. Because God's chariots are invisible and intangible, it is hard for us to believe they are there.

When we try to reach spiritual heights with chariots of our own choosing, God often has to destroy them all before He can bring us to the point of entering *His* chariot. Often a Christian depends too much upon a particular friend for spiritual support, and the Lord is obliged to separate him from that friend. Another may feel that his spiritual health is dependent upon the ministry of his pastor, and this man accepts a call to another church. Some Christians look upon a prayer group or Bible class as the chief source of their spiritual strength; eventually they may find themselves providentially hindered from attending such meetings.

These very deprivations are chariots sent by God to carry His children to the spiritual heights they sought to achieve through these human means. Many of us have to be brought to the end of all human resources before we are willing to say, "Jesus only." We say, "Jesus and my experiences," or "Jesus and my Christian fellowship," or "Jesus and my church work." Until all that comes after the *and* has been taken away from us or proved useless, we will not come to the point of relying solely on Jesus. As long as visible chariots are at hand, we are not willing to trust the invisible ones.

Be thankful, then, for every trial that helps to destroy your earthly chariots and makes you take refuge in the chariot of God. That chariot is ready and waiting for you in every event and circumstance of life. When you finally come to the point of climbing into it, your destination is secured; for no obstacle can hinder God's purpose. Whatever losses or seeming tragedies it takes to bring you to this point are actually gains.

Paul understood this spiritual principle, and he gloried in the losses that brought him such unspeakable rewards.

> . . . I reckon everything as complete loss for the
> sake of what is so much more valuable, the
> knowledge of Christ Jesus my Lord. For his sake I
> have thrown everything away; I consider it all as
> mere garbage, so that I may gain Christ and be
> completely united with him . . . .
>
> Philippians 3:8, 9 TEV

Even the "thorn in the flesh," the messenger of Satan sent
to harass him (2 Corinthians 12:7), became a chariot of
God to Paul, carrying him to spiritual heights that he could
have reached in no other way. By being content with his
weaknesses and trials, Paul was strengthened by them (2
Corinthians 12:10).

As a boy, Joseph had a revelation of his future triumphs
(Genesis 37:5–9); but the circumstances that led to the
fulfillment of his vision looked like veritable steamrollers
of failure and defeat. Slavery and imprisonment are
strange chariots to take one to a kingdom; yet there was no
other way by which Joseph could have been exalted to his
position of high authority in Egypt. God often uses similar
chariots to carry His children to the spiritual thrones He
has waiting for them.

When your trial comes, ask God to open your eyes to see
it as one of His chariots; then ask Him to teach you how to
enter it. Perhaps God did not command or originate the
trial; but the minute you accept it as coming from Him and
put it into His hands, He turns it into a chariot for your
soul. He makes *all* things—even the evil things—work together for good to those who love Him enough to trust His
love (Romans 8:28). Forget about all the "second causes"
and find the Lord in your difficulty. Say, "Lord, open my

eyes, so that I may see this visible enemy as one of your invisible chariots of victory."

The enemy will try to turn your chariot into a steamroller by telling you that God is not in your trouble and that He cannot, or will not, help you. Disregard all such suggestions; overcome them by asserting your confidence in the Lord. Say out loud, "God *is* my refuge and strength, a very present help in trouble" (Psalms 46:1), and "In *every* thing I will give thanks: for this is the will of God in Christ Jesus concerning me" (1 Thessalonians 5:18). Keep repeating these affirmations, no matter how bad the situation may be.

And don't be halfhearted about climbing into your chariot. Resist the temptation to leave one foot dragging on the ground. With no *ifs, buts,* or *supposings,* accept God's will unconditionally and trust His love completely. His "everlasting arms" (Deuteronomy 33:27) are always underneath to support you, in every circumstance and at every moment. Over and over, say to God, "Thy will be done; *Thy* will be done." Shut out every thought except the determination to submit to His will and to trust in His love.

God's will has a place in every trial, and the believer who accepts His will as a chariot will find himself riding upon the heavens with God (Psalms 68:4). From this vantage point, he sees things that are never dreamed of by earthbound souls. The poor victim under the steamroller can see only the dust and stones and the crushing wheel; but the triumphant rider in the chariot sees God working out a divine purpose for his life.

Perhaps you may be wondering where your chariots are to be found. The psalmist speaks of the chariots of God as "twice ten thousand, thousands upon thousands" (Psalms

68:17 RSV). No life lacks God's chariots. If your eyes could be opened today, you would see your home, your place of business, and the streets you drive upon filled with the chariots of God. That cranky neighbor who has made your life miserable and has crushed your spirit like a steamroller—from now on, see her as a chariot sent to carry you to new heights of patience and love. That misunderstanding, that humiliating experience, that unkind word, that disappointment, that loss, that defeat: all these are chariots waiting to carry you to the spiritual victory you have been praying for.

Then mount into them with a thankful heart, and let your acceptance of God's loving will for you carry you safely and triumphantly over all your difficulties.

20
The Life on Wings

Among the many aspects of the "life hid with Christ in God," one that has been of great help to me is what I call the *life on wings.*

Our Lord has told us to consider not only the lilies of the field but also the birds of the air (*see* Matthew 6:26, 28 RSV), and I have found that these little winged creatures have some wonderful lessons for us. Who hasn't at some time echoed the psalmist's cry?

> Oh that I had the wings of a dove to fly away and be at rest! I should escape far away and find a refuge in the wilderness; soon I should find myself a sanctuary from wind and storm.
>
> Psalms 55:6–8 NEB

This yearning for wings is as old as humanity. Our spirits were made to "mount up with wings" (Isaiah 40:31), and they can never be satisfied with an earthbound existence. They are like the captive-born eagle, which chafes at its imprisonment, feeling within itself the instinct of flight, yet hardly knowing what it longs for. We can never rest on earth, and we long to fly away from all that hampers and imprisons us here.

In most cases, the restlessness and discontent express themselves in a search for ways to escape from our outward circumstances. Not realizing that our only way of escape is to mount up with wings, we try to "flee upon horses" (Isaiah 30:16), just as the Israelites did before the fall of Jerusalem.

Our "horses" are the worldly avenues of escape: entertainment, human companionship, travel, a new job, a new marriage. We mount on these and run off in all directions—anywhere to get away from our trouble. But as we should have learned by now, none of these diversions can give peace to our souls. The spirit is not made so that it can flee upon horses; it must always make its flight on wings.

Furthermore, as the Israelites soon discovered, these "horses" generally carry us out of one trouble only to land us in another, ". . . as when a man runs from a lion, and a bear meets him, or turns into a house and leans his hand on the wall, and a snake bites him" (Amos 5:19 NEB). How often have you run from some "lion" in your pathway, only to be met by a "bear"? How many times have you hidden in a "safe" place, only to be bitten by a "serpent"? When will you learn that it is impossible to escape from your troubles by running to some earthly refuge?

Then is there *no* way of escape from trouble? Must we just plod wearily through our trials, being overwhelmed by them at every turn? I rejoice to answer that a glorious way of escape has been provided for every one of us. All we have to do is to mount up on wings and fly away to God. The way of escape does not lie to the east or west, north or south, but upward. "They that wait upon the Lord shall renew their strength; they shall mount up with wings as eagles . . ." (Isaiah 40:31).

Birds, if only they fly high enough, can escape from every snare that is set for them; and the Christian who uses his spiritual wings can also find a sure way of escape from everything that threatens to harm his spirit.

You may be wondering, "What *are* these spiritual wings?" Their secret is found in the phrase, "They that wait upon the Lord." To wait upon God is to be *entirely* surrendered to Him, to trust Him *perfectly*. Therefore we might name our wings *surrender* and *trust*. The Christian who learns the secrets of absolute surrender and perfect trust will be able to mount up on these wings to the "heavenly places in Christ" (Ephesians 1:3), where no earthly annoyance or sorrow has the power to disturb him.

This spiritual plane of life—the "life hid with Christ in God"—is completely independent of circumstances. No cage can imprison and no shackles can bind the believer whose wings have carried him to this height. His view of life and all its experiences is totally different from that of the Christian whose mind is fixed on things here on earth (*see* Colossians 3:2 TEV).

The caterpillar crawling on the ground has a very limited and uninspiring view of its surroundings. How different the world appears to that same caterpillar when it develops wings and, as a butterfly, soars above the very places where it once crawled.

During a winter I spent in London, the sun was obscured for three long months by smoke that hung over the city like a pall. On many days, however, I could see that the sun was shining above the smog. Once or twice, through a rift, I had a glimpse of a bird soaring high above, with sunshine on its wings. There are not enough brushes in London to sweep away the fog; but the bird whose wings can carry him high enough is able to ascend at will out of the gloom below into the sunlight above.

When Habakkuk declared that he would "rejoice in the Lord" and "joy in the God of [his] salvation" even though utter desolation should come upon the earth (Habakkuk 3:18), his soul was surely on wings. And Paul, because he knew how to use his wings, could rejoice even when he was sorrowful (2 Corinthians 6:10). All might be dark on the earthly plane, but to both Paul and the prophet, the heavenly plane was bright with sunshine.

The Bible has much to say about overcoming. (*See* 1 John 5:4; Revelation 2:7, 11, 17, 26; 3:5, 12, 21; 21:7.) Just as birds overcome the lower law of gravity by the higher laws governing flight, so the spirit on wings overcomes the lower "law of sin and death" by the higher "law of the Spirit of life in Christ Jesus" (Romans 8:2). Rising on the wings of surrender and trust into the upper regions of this life in Christ, the believer becomes "more than conqueror" (Romans 8:37) over the bondage produced by the law of sin and death.

Why, then, is triumphant living not a characteristic of *all* Christians? My answer is that a great many Christians never even try their wings. Instead of rising above their circumstances on the wings of trust and surrender, they try to fight them on the earthly plane. On this level the spirit is powerless, and instead of overcoming its difficulties, it is overcome by them and crushed under them.

In describing three of our mutual acquaintances, a friend used the following illustration: "If they should all three come to a spiritual mountain," she said, "Jean would tunnel through it by sheer grit and determination; Barbara would meander around it and eventually find her way to the other side; but Daphne would just flap her wings and fly right over it."

These different ways of coping with problems are perhaps familiar to you. If in the past you have tried to blast a tunnel through the difficulties that stood in your path or have just meandered around them, I hope that in the future you will spread your wings of trust and surrender and soar into the clear atmosphere of God's presence. From that perspective, the steepest mountains dwindle into insignificance.

Even an eagle, however, has to spread its wings and *use* them in order to fly. The largest wings ever known cannot lift a bird one inch off the ground unless they are used. Just so, we Christians must use our spiritual wings if they are to do us any good.

What the believer needs is not more wings, but the courage to try those that he has. The power to surrender and trust exists in every human soul. With these two wings we can mount up to God at any moment—but only if we use them. Merely *wanting* to use them is not enough; we must *do* so, definitely and actively. A theoretical surrender or an occasional moment of trust is ineffective. We must definitely and practically surrender to God each detail of daily life as it comes to us, and trust Him to work them all together for our good (Romans 8:28).

We must meet our hurts, our disappointments, our frustrations, the malice of our enemies, the provoking habits of our friends—our trials and temptations of every sort—with an attitude of active and practical surrender and trust. Only then will we be able to spread our wings and fly above them all to the "heavenly places in Christ." From that vantage point we will be able to see our problems through the eyes of Jesus, and they will lose their power to harm or distress us.

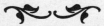

How different the church would be if we Christians learned to cope with our problems in human relationships by using our wings of surrender and trust! Instead of stirring up strife and bitterness by returning evil for evil, we would simply surrender our grievances to God and trust Him to deal with our offending brother or sister. Mounting up on our wings, we would see the problem from Christ's perspective of love and compassion.

Our spirits were made to live in this upper atmosphere and they cannot attain their full potential on any lower level. For this reason, our loving Father plans our lives so that we have ample opportunity to practice flying. In Deuteronomy we are given a picture of God's flying lessons.

> Like an eagle that stirs up its nest, that flutters
> over its young, spreading out its wings, catching
> them, bearing them on its pinions, the Lord alone
> did lead him, and . . . . made him ride on the
> high places of the earth . . . .
>
>   32:11–13 RSV

The mother eagle teaches her little ones to fly by stirring up their nest, making it so uncomfortable that they are forced to leave it and commit themselves to their untried wings. And that's just the way God treats His children. He stirs up our comfortable nests and actually pushes us over the edges of them, so that we are forced to use our wings in an effort to save ourselves.

Look at your problems in this light, and accept with thankfulness every situation that forces you to use your wings. Only with use can they grow strong enough to carry you to the "heavenly places in Christ." Unused muscles gradually atrophy, and if nothing in our lives made it necessary for us to use our wings, we might eventually lose all capacity to fly.

There are, to be sure, conditions that make flight impossible, even for a bird whose wings are strong and who is trying hard to use them. It may be imprisoned in a cage, tethered to the ground with a cord, or entrapped in the "snare of the fowler" (Psalms 91:3). Similar conditions in the spiritual realm may make it impossible for the spirit to soar, until the mighty power of God has set it free.

One snare that entraps many Christians is doubt. As I said in chapter nine, where this difficulty was discussed more fully, many doubts come under the guise of humility and look so plausible that Christians walk into the snare without even recognizing their danger. Then suddenly they find themselves caught and unable to use their wings. Flying is just as impossible for the doubting spirit as it is for the bird caught in the fowler's snare.

The reason is obvious. Two wings are needed to lift a bird or a Christian above the things of earth, and one of our wings—the wing of trust—is disabled by doubt. If you have ever watched a bird with a broken wing trying to fly, you know how ineffective all one-sided flying must be. Unless we use both our wings, we needn't try to fly at all. No matter how vigorously we use the wing of surrender, we will never rise far from the earth as long as the wing of trust is caught in the snare of doubt.

For some believers, the "snare of the fowler" may be a subtle form of sin or a lack of consecration. Where this is the case, the wing of surrender is disabled and flying is still impossible.

Perhaps you feel that your spirit is in a prison from

which it cannot escape, even on wings. No earthly bars, however, can ever imprison the spirit, any more than a cage without a top can hold an eagle in captivity. The only thing that can really imprison an eagle, or the spirit of man, is something that hinders its upward flight. As Isaiah tells us, "it is your iniquities that raise a barrier between you and your God, because of your sins he has hidden his face so that he does not hear you" (Isaiah 59:2 NEB). If you have allowed some sin to build a barrier between you and the Lord, you will not be able to fly until you confess and renounce it.

If you are conscious of no sin in your life, it may be that, without your awareness, your spirit is tethered to something of earth. Friends of mine once hired a rowboat to explore one of the Norwegian fjords. In spite of their vigorous rowing, the boat made no headway until one of them suddenly realized that it was still moored to the dock. "No wonder we couldn't get anywhere," he exclaimed. "We were trying to pull the whole continent of Europe with us!"

Our Lord gave His disciples many warnings about the danger of letting worldly concerns take priority over their discipleship. In one of His parables (Luke 14:16–24) He listed some of the excuses given by guests who were invited to a banquet. One had bought a piece of ground; another, some new cattle. A third had recently married. They all felt that their new responsibilities were more important than the feast prepared for them.

Families, possessions, real estate, or even much more insignificant things may be cords that tether the spirit to earth and keep it from flying. As long as we allow worldly concerns and anxieties to weight us down, our souls will be unable to rise any higher than an eagle with a two-ton boulder tied to its feet. Let us cut every such cord and remove every barrier erected by sin, so that our spirits may be free to "mount up with wings as eagles."

I need to warn you against one mistake, however. The flying I have been talking about isn't necessarily accompanied by joyous emotions or exhilaration. People on emotional highs may not be flying at all. They are like feathers driven upward by a puff of wind, which flutter to the earth as soon as the wind dies down.

The flying I have in mind is a matter of *principle*, not *emotion*. While it may be accompanied by feelings of great joy, it doesn't depend on these feelings. It depends only upon the facts of entire surrender and absolute trust. If you will persist in using these two wings, you will soon find that, regardless of your feelings, your spirit *has* mounted up to heavenly places.

For the promise is sure: "They that wait upon the Lord . . . *shall* mount up with wings as eagles." Not *may* but *shall*. Life on wings is the inevitable result of total surrender and absolute trust. I pray that each one of you will prove it for yourself.